RICHARD II

MARY H. SCANLAN
ASSOCIATE PROFESSOR OF ENGLISH
SETON HALL UNIVERSITY

Macmillan General Reference
A Prentice Hall Macmillan Company
15 Columbus Circle
New York, NY 10023

Copyright © 1964 by
Simon & Schuster, Inc.

All rights reserved. No part of this book
may be reproduced in any form without
permission in writing from the publisher.

MACMILLAN is a registered trademark of Macmillan, Inc.
Monarch and colophons are trademarks of Simon & Schuster, Inc.,
registered in the U.S. Patent and Trademark Office.

ISBN: 0-671-00641-X

Library of Congress Catalog Card Number: 65-7214

Printed in the United States of America

CONTENTS

Introduction	5
Genealogical Table	12
Notes to Table	13
Brief Summary of the Play	13
Detailed Summary of the Play	16
Character Analyses	70
Critical Commentary	79
Essay Questions and Answers	8
Bibliography and Guide to Research	92

INTRODUCTION

SHAKESPEARE'S YOUTH. When an infant son, their first boy but third child, was born late in April, 1564, to John and Mary Arden Shakespeare, they were, of course, unaware that they should make a special effort to record his birthday for posterity. As a result, no one now knows the date of William Shakespeare's birth. This lack of information about his birth date is typical of our sparse knowledge of his whole life story. There are many gaps in Shakespeare's biography. Actually we know less about him than we do about Chaucer, who is two centuries further removed from us. His baptism day, which was probably no more than a week after his birth, is recorded in the parish church, where you may still see the Latin entry in faded ink for the date April 26, 1564. It reads: "Gulielmus filius Johannes Shakspere," (William son of John Shakspere).

John Shakespeare was a fairly prosperous businessman of the town of Stratford, on the Avon River in western England. He also held a series of town offices including the very important positions of high bailiff and chief alderman. Stratford was a busy town in Shakespeare's youth, but a small one. It had only one school, but, as it happened, a very good one. We assume that Shakespeare attended it for the normal length of time, about six or seven years. Like most schools of the day, the Stratford Grammar School emphasized literature. In the brief period of his attendance, Shakespeare would have learned to read and write English, then Latin, and finally he would have received some instruction in Greek. It was a limited but intensive curriculum, and it stood Shakespeare in good stead when he turned to his own writing. But he was not to be a writer for a while yet. He was married at eighteen to twenty-six-year-old Anne Hathaway, daughter of a well-to-do farmer of the area. Susanna, the first child, was born six months after the marriage, and the twins, Hamnet and Judith, were two years younger. The disparity in age beween William and Anne, Susanna's birth date, and Shakespeare's long residence in London away from his family, who apparently remained in Stratford—all these facts have led to the assumption by many that Shakespeare's marriage was an unhappy one. After the birth of the twins in 1585, we have no record of Shakespeare and his activities (aside from a very brief court reference) until 1592. We do not know what work he did while living in Stratford, nor how, nor when, nor why he went to London. Various traditional stories deal with this period, among them one that he was a schoolmaster for a while before leaving Stratford.

HIS PROFESSIONAL CAREER. It is reasonable to assume that Shakespeare went to London in the late 1580's when he was in his middle twenties. In 1592, a London dramatist, obviously jealous of the "upstart crow" from the country, referred to Shakespeare as an established London actor and playwright. Already the man from Stratford had made a name for himself in the theatrical world of the metropolis. He remained in London until about 1612, when he returned to Stratford-on-Avon. During these twenty-five years of London residence, he had a rather modest career as an actor. But as a dramatist, he was almost as great a success with his contemporaries as he has been with posterity. He composed for his approving public thirty-seven plays, and, in addition, wrote a set of one hundred and fifty-four sonnets and several other poems. He also showed considerable business acumen. He was a "sharer" member of the acting company known as the Lord Chamberlain's Men. (After 1603, they were called the King's Men.) This became the most popular and prosperous of the London theatrical companies. Shakespeare's share of their earnings would have been substantial, particularly after they built, in 1599, their own theater, the famous Globe. Although never extremely wealthy, Shakespeare did become a man of substantial means. He died on April 23, 1616, and was buried in the same Stratford parish church that he was taken to as a baby for baptism.

SHAKESPEARE'S PLAYS. Shakespeare wrote almost forty plays. The famous *First Folio*, the first collected edition of his plays, was published in 1623 by two of his friends from the King's Men. They included thirty-six plays, and critics today think that at least one more, *Pericles*, should be added to the Folio contents. It is probable that Shakespeare wrote parts of other plays; collaboration was very common in the production of Renaissance English drama. So we are not sure of Shakespeare's total output. Neither are we sure about the chronological sequence of his works; few Shakespearian scholars care to be dogmatic about exact dating for the plays. But a generally accepted chronological arrangement has been arrived at on the basis of information provided by both external and internal evidence. Examples of external evidence would be contemporary references to performances of the plays in letters, diaries, literary criticism, etc. Examples of internal evidence would be references in the plays themselves to datable historical events, and variation in style and versification. On the basis of such evidence, it is possible to divide Shakespeare's dramatic career into three stages.

1) *The Early Plays:* These are the plays of Shakespeare's first decade of dramatic writing, approximately 1590 to 1600. They include comedies, like *Midsummer Night's Dream* and *Merchant of Venice*, and all the chronicle plays except the very late *Henry VIII*. In this group there are also three tragedies (not counting the chronicle tragedies): the poor *Titus Andronicus, Romeo and Juliet, and Julius Caesar*. This is sometimes called Shakespeare's apprentice period. He was learning his "trade" during this decade, and he learned rapidly. This rapid development is apparent to anyone who turns from the rather vapid and inane *Lover's Labour's Lost* to the antic but meaningful *Twelfth Night*, or from the almost ludicrously bloody and blustering *Titus Andronicus* to the thoughtful, moving tragedy of Caesar and Brutus. The same type of development is to be seen in the histories. This is also called the lyrical period. All the plays of this decade are rich, some, like *Romeo and Juliet* and *Richard II*, probably too rich in imagery and word-melody. Shakespeare had to learn during this period how to reconcile and combine his lyrical and dramatic talents.

2) *Major Plays:* The next decade, 1600 to 1610, produced the masterpieces. With only a couple of exceptions, the plays are tragedies. Those exceptions, *All's Well That Ends Well* and *Measure for Measure*, are almost as dark with crime and suffering as the tragedies. They do end happily, but they leave their readers apprehensive and dubious about human nature. The tragedies include Shakespeare's most famous four: *Hamlet, Othello, King Lear* and *Macbeth*, probably written in that order. In these and in the minor tragedies of the period, like *Antony and Cleopatra and Coriolanus*, Shakespeare probes the nature and effects of evil more deeply than any other writer of the Christian era. He presents clearly his concept of tragedy; all these tragic heroes are self-ruined. These plays inspire a full measure of the fear and pity Aristotle finds in great tragedy. But they are also reassuring; Shakespeare implies that there is a basic sanity and significance to the universe and to human life. After the turmoil of each hero's tragic career, the world of his survivors is able to subside back to sane normalcy.

3) *The Final Plays:* These last works, *Cymbeline, The Winter's Tale* and *The Tempest*, are of special interest. They are outlandishly romantic in their settings, and yet they present problems of everyday life, such as quarrels between relatives and friends, rivalry and jealousy, cynicism and suspicion. But all the problems are solved; serenity and peacefulness warm the concluding scenes of each of these plays. If, as some believe, Shakespeare's great tragedies were written in a period of personal gloom and depression, he apparently made his way through that dark night. When it was behind him, he found that he had a new understanding of life to express in his final plays. He seems content that good can surmount evil, that the human condition can be a happy one.

SHAKESPEARE'S THEATER. The theater for which Shakespeare wrote his plays was quite different from our typical modern theater buildings. The usual Renaissance English theater was a circular or polygonal structure surrounding a large, unroofed courtyard. The stage, a rather low platform, projected out into the courtyard, opposite the public entrance. Frequently, the stage had two levels: the main platform and above it a gallery that could be used when the action occurred in elevated places, like the ramparts of a castle or the balcony outside Juliet's room. Behind the main stage there might be a curtained recess, useful when an inner room was indicated, or perhaps a cave or hiding place. The acting companies of Shakespeare's day liked colorful costumes (usually typical Renaissance dress, no matter what historical period the play was set in) and made considerable use of properties; but they did not attempt much scenery. The dramatist wove into his speeches sufficient description to stimulate the audience to imagine the appropriate scenery. This Renaissance audience was both less and more fortunate than the modern audience. Physically, they were less fortunate. Most of them stood on the bare earth of the "pit," the unroofed courtyard around the stage. To escape this jostling, unruly, rough crowd, some of the wealthier patrons paid a higher fee and climbed up into the rather rickety balconies that overlooked the courtyard and stage. Here they enjoyed more privacy and also some protection from the weather. But their comfort was only comparative; even *their* accommodations would seem pretty crude to a modern theater-goer. However, what they lacked in physical comfort, they made up for in the intensity and vividness of their theater experience. Theirs was a very intimate theater. The audience was close physically to the stage action, and, when their attention was caught, very close psychologically. To a greater extent than is usually possible today, the gifted writer and actor could experience the thrill of really capturing his audience and drawing them out of their habitual selves and worlds into the new world of the action on the stage. This feeling of close fellowship with a very responsive public probably inspired some of Shakespeare's best dramatic writing. The Renaissance productions were speedy. Usually there was no interval dividing acts and scenes. The whole action flowed uninterruptedly across the stage. Most of the theater buildings were equipped to give daytime performances only. Since just the balconies and stage were roofed, and they rather inadequately, performances were cancelled in bad weather. The majority of the theaters were located in the suburb of Southwark, just across the Thames River from London proper. On a fair afternoon, when neither plague nor political unrest had suspended theatrical activity, the Thames would be busy with small boats ferrying Londoners over the water to the theaters. On the rooftops of the playhouses offering programs that day, flags waved and, as the hour approached, a bugle blew to hurry the latecomers. In this fashion one day in 1595 or 1596, Londoners flocked to see a new play by Master Shakespeare, a play about an unhappy king who had died two centuries before, a play about Richard II.

THE TRAGEDY OF KING RICHARD THE SECOND. *Richard II,* the short title usually adopted for this play, is both a tragedy and a chronicle or history play. Shakespeare wrote two sets of chronicle plays, known as "tetralogies" because each is made up of four plays. *Richard II* is the first play in the first tetralogy ("first" historically speaking; actually, Shakespeare wrote this tetralogy after the other one; so it is referred to as *his* second tetralogy). It is followed by *Henry IV, Part 1* and *Part 2,* and by *Henry V.* The other tetralogy is composed of the three parts of *Henry VI* and *Richard III.* The two sets cover approximately one century, the fifteenth, a troubled and interesting period in English history. *Richard II,* like almost all the chronicle plays, was written in Shakespeare's early period. It is therefore not a product of his mature genius. It has faults in plot, characterization, and style. Although not a great play, it is a good one. It poses a recurring political problem, and it presents a complex hero. It gives evidence of Shakespeare's powers at a crucial stage in his dramatic development.

HISTORICAL BACKGROUND. The historical Richard II or Richard of Bordeaux (he was born in that French town) became king of England as a boy of ten. He succeeded his grandfather, Edward III. Edward had a long (1327-1377) and fairly successful reign. He and his wife, the Flemish Philippa, had seven sons and five daughters. The eldest son and heir to the throne was Edward, the Black Prince, a popular figure who distinguished himself in the early stages of the One Hundred Years War with France.

Other sons were Lionel, Duke of Clarence (who does not figure in the play because he died in 1368); John of Gaunt, Duke of Lancaster (born in Ghent in his mother's native Flanders), Edmund of Langley, Duke of York; and Thomas of Woodstock, Duke of Gloucester.

Unfortunately, the Black Prince predeceased his father; he died in 1376, and Edward III died in 1377. The throne then went to the Black Prince's small son Richard. Various regency councils handled the affairs of the realm during the boy's minority. When Richard was only fourteen, he distinguished himself in a national emergency, the Peasant's Revolt. At the height of this destructive and frightening uprising, Richard rode out of London and fearlessly interviewed and quieted the insurgents. But the promise of mature strength that his youthful accomplishment offered was never realized. Richard was a failure as a king, partly because of other people and partly because of himself. In 1389, when he was twenty-two, he finally forced his advisors to allow him to really rule; but he always had to contend with the family animosities and intrigues, and with the ambitions of his uncles and cousins, especially John of Gaunt and Thomas of Woodstock. Added to that, he was of a nature to be more impressed with the privileges than the responsibilities of monarchy. He had little talent for either military or administrative leadership. He married twice. His first wife, the popular Anne of Bohemia, shared his love of art and gaiety, but also exerted some stabilizing influence on the unsteady king. She died of the plague in 1394, after twelve years of marriage. In 1396, Richard married Isabelle, a French Princess, a child of seven or eight. Public discontent with Richard's rule grew increasingly strong in the 1390's. Henry of Bolingbroke, Gaunt's son, emerged as the strongest leader of the opposition party. He finally forced the resignation of Richard in 1399, and supplanted him on the throne. Richard was imprisoned first in the Tower of London and later at Pontefract (Pomfret) Castle in Yorkshire. He died there in February, 1400. Historians are convinced that he was murdered, probably by starvation. There were also rumors that a minor courtier, Sir Pierce of Exton, had attacked and killed him in his cell. Almost immediately a kind of glamorous mystery drifted around Richard, and there were even reports that he had not died but had escaped to a life of anonymity in Scotland. In point of fact, however, he did die at Pontefract. He lies now, beside Anne of Bohemia, in a beautiful tomb in Westminster Abbey. On the tomb is the very appropriate epitaph "Fuisse felicem miserrimum," (To have been fortunate was most miserable). Richard has come down in history as a weak, perhaps at the end even deranged, monarch, but as May McKisack observes in *The Fourteenth Century* "something of his charm has survived the centuries." Shakespeare faithfully represents this character ambiguity or complexity.

SOURCES OF RICHARD II. For all his chronicle plays and for sections of some of his other plays also, Shakespeare relied heavily on what one critic has called his favorite book, *The Chronicles of England, Scotland, and Ireland* by Raphael Holinshed (pronounced Hol' inz hed). A second and enlarged edition of this work appeared very conveniently for Shakespeare in 1586-7. Shakespeare follows Holinshed, often quite closely, for almost all the main episodes of this play. He obviously had *The Chronicles* right at his elbow as he wrote. It is an instructive experience to place passages from *The Chronicles* beside parallel sections of *Richard II*, and to observe how Shakespeare's genius breathed life into a rather routine historical account. As J. Dover Wilson says, "Holinshed furnishes the plain hempen warp upon which the colorful tapestry we call *Richard II* was woven." Shakespeare also looked into three or four other works, some French and some English, for information about Richard and his times. He probably had the benefit of an earlier play, *Woodstock,* which dealt with the murder of Thomas, Duke of Gloucester. Shakespeare may have acted in that play or seen it presented. Some think that he also had as guide another play about Richard II by some earlier dramatist. If such a play existed, it suffered the fate of many minor Renaissance plays and vanished from sight. Almost certainly *Richard II* owes something to Christopher Marlowe's play about King Edward II. Edward II was Richard's great-grandfather, and there is some similarity in their careers.

Since he was writing drama and not history, Shakespeare did not feel bound to follow exactly the facts he found in history books. Whether or not he was acquainted with Aristotle's famous distinction that history relates what *did* happen (the particular) and drama what *may* happen (the universal), he certainly believed in it. He was not writing exactly what did happen in one set of months to a king named Richard, but rather what always does happen to a personality of the type he felt Richard possessed. Therefore, he made some interesting modifications in his source facts, and he improvised some original material.

Outstanding in his modifications is his characterization of the Queen. Historically Richard's queen in 1598-9 was the child Isabelle, daughter of the King of France. She was only about eight years old and quite removed from all the political and personal turmoil of her husband's last years. Shakespeare makes her a young woman, in love with her husband, and of some mild significance in the political events. The relationship which he suggests between her and Richard is probably transferred from the very happy marriage of Richard and his first wife, Anne of Bohemia. Since his point is that Richard, for all his faults, had been loved by a lovely person, Shakespeare probably felt justified in a little juggling of dates and personages to show this love in his play. And, of course, he *was* justified. The deposition scene (Act 4) is quite different from the actual historical event. Shakespeare has coalesced here several Parliamentary sessions, and the real Richard's resignation was tendered in the Tower of London, not before a large body in Westminster Hall.

There are also minor alterations. The Duchess of York was really Aumerle's stepmother, but for dramatic tension Shakespeare makes her his mother. There is a trace of the true relationship in the Duchess' reminder to York that the young man resembles his father closely and herself not at all. The other duchess, Gloucester's widow, did not die at the time and place Shakespeare indicates. He also changed some of the characters' ages. Prince Hal, who is reported as leading a life of profligacy, was actually a lad of twelve at this time. "Young" Harry Percy, on the other hand, was a mature man, older than either Richard or Bolingbroke. There is, as would be expected, some syncopation of time. For instance, Bolingbroke's return from exile seems to follow much more closely on his father's death than it actually did. The historical events depicted in the play began in April, 1398, and ended in February, 1400, but Shakespeare's handling of his material creates the illusion of a much briefer period.

Shakespeare also made some notable original contributions to the story of Richard's life. He invented the conversation between Gaunt and the Duchess of Gloucester (Act 1, Scene 2), Gaunt's deathbed scene (Act 2, Scene 1), the imaginative episode in the garden at Langley with the Queen and the gardeners (Act 3, Scene 4), the parting of Richard and his Queen (Act 5, Scene 1), the pleading of the Duchess of York for her son (Act 5, Scene 3), Richard's prison soliloquy (Act 5, Scene 5), and the presentation of Richard's coffin to King Henry (Act 5, Scene 6). These are all famous passages, and most of them are admired. We feel a special zest and enthusiasm in them, as if Shakespeare was glad of the freedom they afforded his imagination, which was somewhat curbed and restrained in other scenes where he had to follow his sources.

The source situation for *Richard II* is typical of Shakespeare's procedure in his other plays. He likes to start with an already formulated plot (in the case of the chronicle plays, this "plot" was real life as recorded by history), and then to transform and universalize its ingredients by the magic of his special artistic alchemy.

GENEALOGICAL TABLE FOR CHIEF CHARACTERS IN RICHARD II

King Edward III
1312-1377
r. 1327-1377

Edward
The Black Prince
1330-1376

King Richard II
1367-1400
r. 1377-1399
m. 1. Anne of Bohemia
d. 1394
2. Isabelle of France
d. 1409

Lionel
Duke of Clarence
1338-1368

Philippa
d. 1391

Roger
d. 1398

Edmund Mortimer
d. 1424

John of Gaunt
Duke of Lancaster
1340-1398

King Henry IV
Bolingbroke
1366-1413
r. 1399-1413

King Henry V
1388-1422
r. 1413-1422

Edmund
Duke of York
1341-1402
m. 1. Isabel of Castile
d. 1393
2. Joan Holland
d. 1434

Edward
Duke of Aumerle
1373-1415

Thomas
Duke of Gloucester
1355-1397
m. Eleanor Bohum
d. 1399

Anne
d. 1438

NOTES TO GENEALOGICAL TABLE

1) The abbreviations d., m., r. mean died, married, reigned, respectively.

2) King Edward III had seven sons, but two, both named William, died in infancy.

3) Richard II had no children. His heir presumptive, Roger Mortimer, predeceased Richard by one year. When Richard died, Edmund Mortimer, great-grandson of Lionel, had a better claim to the throne than did his cousin Bolingbroke.

4) Historically, the mother of Aumerle was Isabel of Castile who died before the events of the play. The Duchess of York at the time covered by the play was Joan Holland. Shakespeare combines the two women for his character of the Duchess of York.

5) In the Wars of the Roses, the Lionel and Edmund lines unite to become the York faction (White Rose) which battles John's line, the Lancaster faction (Red Rose), for the throne. Finally, at the Battle of Bosworth Field, 1485, Henry VII overcomes Richard III, seizes the throne and establishes the Tudor line. Henry VII was descended from French royalty and the Welsh Tudors on his father's side, and on his mother's side he was descended from John of Gaunt. John first married Blanche, the mother of Bolingbroke. His final marriage was to Katharine Swynford, Chaucer's sister-in-law. His children by her had been born out of wedlock, but were later legitimatized. They had the family name of Beaufort. It was from this Beaufort branch that Henry VII, the first Tudor king, was descended. He, of Lancaster descent, married Elizabeth of York and so joined the White and Red Roses into the famous double Tudor Rose.

BRIEF SUMMARY OF RICHARD II

King Richard II ruled medieval England from 1377 to 1399. The play begins in the last year of his reign. Richard has not been a successful king, and the powerful nobility of the land, particularly his own uncles and cousins, are now getting out of hand. At the play's opening, Richard is about to summon to his presence one of the strongest of those cousins, Henry, Duke of Hereford (Bolingbroke). Bolingbroke has brought serious charges of graft, murder, and treason against Thomas Mowbray, Duke of Norfolk. Mowbray, who has made countercharges against Bolingbroke, is also summoned. After the two noblemen repeat their accusations, Richard attempts to make peace. He is unable either to force or persuade the men to obey his royal will; so, reluctantly, he appoints the date and place for the mortal combat or judicial duel that will decide the issue. One of the crimes Bolingbroke accuses Mombray of committing is the murder of the Duke of Gloucester, uncle of both Richard and Bolingbroke. The Duke's widow now visits Bolingbroke's father, John of Gaunt, who has the title Duke of Lancaster, and complains that little has been done to avenge her husband. Gaunt, a seasoned courtier and politician, implies that the King himself arranged the murder. Gaunt is a man of forceful, haughty character, but he is also a believer in the Divine Right of Kings. Therefore, he is reluctant to move against the King. The appointed day for the duel arrives. Just as Bolingbroke and Mowbray are about to begin combat, Richard halts the proceedings. He announces that Bolingbroke and Mowbray are to go forthwith into exile, Mowbray for life and Bolingbroke for six years.

Bolingbroke's departure into exile is marked by a great demonstration by the common people who like and admire him. Richard is irked by this, but gives his mind to his own departure to Ireland to put down a rebellion there. To finance this, he will continue the oppressive taxation and other unsound fiscal policies that have displeased his people. In the midst of his departure plans he gets news of the serious illness of Gaunt and goes to visit him, hoping that Gaunt will die. Gaunt, after a splendid tribute to England, sternly rebukes his nephew Richard for misgovernment. But this exhausts him and a few minutes later he dies. Richard immediately seizes the Lancaster properties which should go to Bolingbroke. His other uncle, the Duke of York, protests. Richard ignores his advice, but does appoint him his deputy for the duration of the Irish campaign. After Richard's departure, the Earl of Northumberland confides to two other nobles who are as angered as he by Richard's highhandedness that Bolingbroke has decided to return secretly from exile in France. They all decide to join Bolingbroke in the north; so Richard's reign is threatened by a conspiracy of disaffected nobles.

Richard's Queen, who remains in England, is frightened by a premonition of trouble. This premonition proves well grounded as reports of the growing success of the conspiracy pour in to the kingless court. A message is sent to Richard, but the Channel winds will delay his return. York is too old and too indecisive to handle the emergency well. Most of the high nobles defect to Bolingbroke. Even Richard's intimate associates, the lesser nobles Bushy, Green, and Bagot, think only of their own safety. Bolingbroke and the Earl of Northumberland have joined forces and marched across England to the southwestern coast. There they encounter York and the small band he has mustered. York's resistance to Bolingbroke is limited to some criticism of him as a usurper. As far as action goes, he takes the easy course and joins Bolingbroke. Next, a contingent of Welsh soldiers, a troop very important to Richard, gives up waiting for him and goes over to Bolingbroke. This landslide of events disastrous to Richard continues. Bolingbroke captures Bristol Castle, a stronghold of Richard's, and executes its occupants, who include Bushy and Green. Richard finally arrives in England and lands on the Welsh coast, not far from the insurgents' base. As he talks to his cousin, the Duke of Aumerle, and to the Bishop of Carlisle and hears reports of reverses on his side, he displays great changeability in his reaction to his perilous situation. At one moment he is jubilantly and foolishly confident that God will protect him, the divinely ordained king. At the next, he is mired in despair, ready to succumb to Bolingbroke. He vacillates between these two extremes, but the pessimistic reaction is dominant. Richard's personality, his political theory and policies, his very talents (artistic and intellectual) all make him unfit for kingship. We begin to feel some pity for him.

Richard and Bolingbroke meet soon at Flint Castle. Richard, on the ramparts, hears the demands of Bolingbroke, who is in the courtyard below, bulwarked by his rebel followers and forces. Bolingbroke wants Richard to revoke his exile sentence and return his property. Richard knows that if he agrees to do this, he is, in effect, abdicating his power and crowning Bolingbroke. But, with almost no resistance, Richard does agree to Bolingbroke's demands. This is the climax of the main conflict in the play: Richard versus Bolingbroke; and Bolingbroke has won. Despite this triumph of the competent man, the play is a tragedy. It is the tragedy of Richard whom fate forced into a position for which he was not fit. It is a tragedy for England, forced to choose between lawful incompetence and unlawful competence. Quickly replacing Richard as the dominant figure, the efficient Bolingbroke decides that everyone should return to London and Westminster. Meanwhile the Queen at a country estate hears of Richard's plight from a gardener's chance remarks and also decides to go to London.

At Westminster, Bolingbroke calls a kind of parliament in which the case of Gloucester's murder is reopened. This time Aumerle is accused, probably because he has been a supporter (although not a strong one) of Richard. The more important business of the assembly is to hear Richard's formal abdication. The Bishop of Carlisle attacks Bolingbroke as a usurper and prophesies calamitous consequences for England. Richard does abdicate but not until he has, in his own imaginative way, impressed on the gathering that this change to a more efficient administrator is being done at the cost of great personal suffering to the *man* Richard and is a risky defiance of the commonly held theory that the reigning king is God's special deputy. The Bishop of Carlisle, the Abbot of Westminster, and Aumerle plot a counter-revolution against Bolingbroke.

Circumstances force Richard and his Queen to bid each other farewell pathetically and publicly on a London street. There they hear Bolingbroke's decision that the Queen must return to her native France and Richard be removed to imprisonment in remote Pomfret Castle, in northern England.

If there is any minor plot in *Richard II*, it is condensed into the brief episode of the York family that now occurs. The Duke and Duchess of York discover that their only son Aumerle is involved in the conspiracy against Bolingbroke. York, terrified for his own precarious standing with Bolingbroke to whom he has now made formal allegiance, rushes off to court to inform against his own son. The Duchess, alarmed for her "child's" safety, also speeds to Westminster to plead for Aumerle. Aumerle himself joins the fast-riding family cavalcade to petition Bolingbroke for forgiveness. The young man rides the fastest and gets a promise of forgiveness from Bolingbroke just before his father arrives and divulges to the new King the full enormity of Aumerle's crime. Then the Duchess bursts in, throws herself at Bolingbroke's feet, a ludicrous, but moving, figure. Bolingbroke rather gracefully (never a real villain, Bolingbroke is increasingly likable in the final scenes) yields to the various pressures exerted by this hectic family scene. Aumerle is forgiven, but the other conspirators are to be overcome and punished.

A minor nobleman, Sir Pierce of Exton, who believes that Bolingbroke would be relieved if Richard were killed, rides north to Pomfret. There, in miserable confinement, Richard communes with himself. We see that he is still the self-centered, discontented, impractical man of the play's beginning, but he has attained some stability and dignity in his misfortune. Our sympathy for him increases as death closes in on him. He has three visitors: the first is a former servant whose brief call is friendly and pitying; the second is his jailer bearing food which Richard refuses to eat because he suspects poison; the third is Exton, accompanied by two thugs. All three attack Richard. He gives a good account of himself but is felled by a blow from Exton.

Back at court, Bolingbroke is pleased by reports of successful suppression of the small revolt against him. He is less pleased, or so he says, by the arrival of Exton whose servants carry in the coffin of Richard. Bolingbroke, far from thanking Exton, exiles him. But he does admit that Richard's death is politically advantageous to him. He announces a period of mourning for the court and vows that he will himself make a penitential pilgrimage to the Holy Land.

DETAILED SUMMARY
Act I: Scene 1

The play begins in the year 1398, at the court of the medieval English King Richard II. This first scene is angry in mood and ominous. Richard is seated on his throne surrounded by courtiers. Peremptorily, he asks his uncle, John of Gaunt, Duke of Lancaster, if Gaunt has brought to court, as he had promised to do, his son and heir, Henry Bolingbroke. Bolingbroke has accused Thomas Mowbray, Duke of Norfolk, of treason.

> **COMMENT:** As dukes, both Bolingbroke and Mowbray belong to the highest level of nobility, but Bolingbroke, because he is of royal blood and heir of John of Gaunt, outranks Mowbray.

This accusation is of the type called an "appeal," a very serious charge which the accuser must stand ready to back up with a duel to the death. Assured by Gaunt that Henry will be there, Richard probes deeper. Has Gaunt discovered Bolingbroke's reason for the accusation? Does he have good grounds? Or is he moved by personal malice and hatred? Gaunt answers respectfully enough, but rather tersely, that he believes his son does have evidence of treachery—treachery threatening the King himself.

RICHARD II

COMMENT: In these first speeches Richard discloses in two small words (and probably unintentionally) his feelings about his two Lancaster relatives. He makes a point of calling Gaunt "old." Gaunt is fifty-eight, and it is true that he considers himself old. In the medieval period the life expectancy span was much briefer than ours; a person over fifty would be considered elderly, equivalent to a man of seventy today. But Richard *wants* to think of him as close to death, for the death of Gaunt will benefit Richard. It will relieve him of his uncle's supervision and interference; it might make it possible for Richard to seize the vast Lancaster lands and revenues. Bolingbroke, on the other hand, Richard calls "bold." Richard already feels a threat to himself in the forceful, "boisterous" nature of his cousin.

Richard orders that both Bolingbroke and Mowbray be called before him. He wants to see them confront each other, "frowning brow to brow," and to hear them speak their grievances freely. He knows that they are both haughty, strong-willed men. They enter together, each making a brief, complimentary speech to the King. Richard is not a good judge of character, but neither is he a complete fool. He, therefore, thanks them for the praise but reminds them that one must be insincere, since each has accused the other of high treason, which would be an offense against the King. (Shakespeare ignores the possibility that they might both be mistaken in their charges and that, therefore, neither would be guilty of treason.)

Both noblemen show themselves to be indeed haughty and high-spirited as they repeat their accusations in the presence of the King. Bolingbroke, who speaks first, is the more aggressive. He calls on Heaven to witness that he is motivated solely by a true subject's love for his ruler's safety and by any "misbegotten hate." Turning to Mowbray, he says he is willing to make good with his body (in combat) the charge he prefers against him. He will even stake his immortal soul on the truth of his words. Then, in indignant tones, he labels Mowbray "traitor" and "miscreant" (criminal). With a verbal cleverness of the type that will be shown many times in this play, he says Mowbray is "too good to be so [too high in rank to be evil], and too bad to live." In pompous righteousness he declares that the higher the title, the more disgraceful any misdeeds that becloud it. He winds up by repeating "traitor," which he says he stuffs down the throat of Mowbray. He then challenges his opponent to single combat. "What my tongue speaks, my right drawn sword may prove."

Mowbray is by no means cowed. His words, he says, may be cold and few, but this is not a woman's war, a verbal squabble. This is a quarrel that must be settled by combat and bloodshed. But he is not so tame as to be completely silent. Only the restraint imposed upon him by the royal presence prevents him from flinging back at Bolingbroke the name of "traitor." He is well aware of the advantage Bolingbroke has in his royal connections and close relationship to Richard. Nevertheless, "I do defy and spit at him / Call him a slanderous coward and a villain." He is glad to accept the challenge of Bolingbroke. In fact, he would "allow him odds," or travel far to meet him, even to the "frozen ridges of the Alps." Mowbray then grasps the pommel of his sword. With this weapon will he defend his loyalty and prove Bolingbroke a most false liar. Bolingbroke immediately throws down his "gage."

> **COMMENT:** The "gage" or pledge to fight is the challenger's glove. He hurls it at the feet of his opponent who shows his acceptance of the challenge by picking up the glove. The single combat was a recognized method of settling quarrels among the nobility. It had judicial force and was usually a fight to the death. The man who won was considered to have had the just case.

Bolingbroke says he'll disavow, in connection with this controversy, all his royal connections and any help they might be to him. He taunts Mowbray with cowardice and dares him, if he isn't too weak with fear, to pick up the gage. Mowbray, of course, snatches it up and declares that he is ready to stand the knightly trial. It he *is* a traitor or if he fights unfairly, let him perish in the encounter.

Richard, who has not been able to get in a word for some time and who finds the situation going far beyond his plans for it, demands that Bolingbroke recite his specific charges against Mowbray, who, Richard points out, has a good record. Thereupon, Bolingbroke supports his statement that Mowbray is a traitor with two specific charges and one general one. The first is that Mowbray misappropriated eight thousand nobles (a gold coin which had the purchasing power of about fifteen dollars today) which he had been instructed to pay to English soldiers fighting in France in a campaign of the Hundred Years War. The second specific charge is that Mowbray had plotted and accomplished the murder of the King's uncle, Thomas of Gloucester (pronounced Glos' ter), uncle also of Bolingbroke himself.

> **COMMENT:** Gloucester had been murdered (his head chopped off) the year before at Calais (pronounced Kah lay'), one of the French towns in English hands. At the time of the murder, Mowbray was in command of the English forces in the town.

Gloucester was as guiltless and as well-meaning as Abel of the Old Testament, and Bolingbroke is determined to avenge him. The general charge is the extravagant claim that all the treasons of the last eighteen years (the period of Richard's effective reign) can be traced back to "false Mowbray."

The King takes a long look at this cocksure Lancaster cousin of his and mutters to himself, "How high a pitch his resolution soars!" But without delay, he turns to Mowbray and invites him to speak out freely and answer the charges. He assures Mowbray that he will not allow his family connection with Bolingbroke to prejudice him; they are both subjects of equal status in his eyes. He swears this by his "scepter's awe," and he refers to his "sacred blood."

COMMENT: Richard touches here upon a theory that both he and Gaunt elaborate later, the theory called the Divine Right of Kings. Note, too, that he stresses a ceremonial symbol of his power.

Mowbray vehemently and circumstantially denies both charges. He is not an embezzler. Three-quarters of the money given him to take to Calais he distributed to the King's soldiers. The remaining quarter he kept by consent (apparently of Richard). The King owed him that amount for the expenses Mowbray suffered when he went to France to escort Richard's present Queen to England for her marriage. So Bolingbroke can just swallow that lie! Furthermore, he did *not* kill Gloucester, although he *should* have. He must admit, however, that he did once attempt to kill Bolingbroke's father. This he does repent; he has confessed it; he has also begged Gaunt's pardon and, with a look at the listening Gaunt, believes he has received it. Otherwise Bolingbroke's charges are the "rancor of a villain . . . and most degenerate traitor." Contemptuously, he throws down his own glove. He asks Richard to assign their trial day.

COMMENT: Which nobleman was telling the truth is never disclosed in the play. Later Gaunt implies that Richard himself planned Gloucester's death. Gloucester, like Richard's other uncles, interfered repeatedly in court affairs. Mowbray seems genuinely loyal to Richard. It is likely that he did carry out orders from Richard for Gloucester's removal.

The King with some help from John of Gaunt, who with the other courtiers has been observing in silence the heated progress of the quarrel, attempts to persuade the two enraged nobles to withdraw their challenges. They should "forget, forgive, . . . and be agreed." He even tries to make a little joke about it. The doctors, consulting the astrology that influenced such medieval medical practice, have said it is not a good month for blood-letting! But the "wrath-kindled gentlemen" do not smile. They remain obdurate, scornful of each other, and, although outwardly respectful, quite unintimidated by the King. Each protests that he cannot in honor withdraw his gage.

Mowbray says that he would give up his life in the King's service, but he cannot, even for his monarch, allow a blemish on his name. He has been wounded by a slanderous attack. The only balm that can heal the wound is the heart-blood of his accuser. A man who has lost his good reputation is but "painted clay." Take away his honor, and he might as well be dead. He implores his liege to let him defend his honor.

Getting nowhere with Mowbray, Richard turns around to Bolingbroke who has already firmly resisted his father's attempts to sway him. He is just as unyielding to Richard. "Oh, God defend my soul from such deep sin!" To withdraw his challenge would shame his family and his noble rank. Before he would agree to forgive Mowbray, he would bite out his tongue and "spit it bleeding . . . / Where shame both harbor, even in Mowbray's face." This violent defiance discourages Richard. He admits defeat and emphasizes his failure with a memorable line, "We were not born to sue, but to command." In obvious displeasure, he orders them to appear on St. Lambert's Day, September 17, at Coventry (in central England) for their single combat.

> **COMMENT:** Although the dissension between the two defiant Dukes captures our attention in this scene, the most meaningful element in the characterization is the contrast shown between the King and his cousin Bolingbroke. The King, despite his regal manner and words, proves ineffectual, unable to curb his unruly subjects. Even in this first scene we see that Richard's kingship is more a matter of externals than real power. He talks in kingly phrases and he performs the ceremonial actions of royalty, but we do not find in him the confidence of real power and authority. Bolingbroke is decisive, persistent, and successful in forcing the issue to single combat. He seems a man of great, but so far unrealized, potential. The King shows that he, too, is aware of this power and rather frightened by it when he describes Bolingbroke with the image drawn from falconry: "How high a pitch his resolution soars!" Falconry (hunting small birds with hawks) was the most popular sport of the day among the nobility. The "pitch" is the highest point in the hawk's flight, the point at which he hovers just before he swoops on his victim. It is, therefore, a very fitting expression for Richard's fears about Bolingbroke.

SUMMARY. This first scene makes the following important points:

1) Richard's rule is threatened by weaknesses in his own character, especially:

a. His inability to control his nobles; that is, his inability to be a *real* king.

b. His excessive reliance on the symbols of his office and the *appearance* of monarchy that they provide. He expects Bolingbroke and Mowbray to defer to him simply because he has the title and office of King. We observe that, despite their polite expressions of deference, they do not have that kind of respect for the kingly office. Richard must show personal strength if he is to dominate.

2) Richard's rule is also threatened by forces outside himself, by:

a. Bolingbroke who has the personal power and leadership ability that Richard lacks.

b. Gaunt who gives his nephew only very limited support.

3) The dispute between the high-ranking nobles, Bolingbroke and Mowbray, was too serious to be resolved by arbitration, even that of the King; it will proceed to armed conflict. Therefore, the danger it threatens to the peace of the realm, far from being lessened, is to be increased.

This scene also introduces the three most important characters in the play: Richard, Bolingbroke, and Gaunt. Of the characters who have not yet appeared, the Queen of England, the Duke of York (Richard's third uncle), and York's son, Aumerle, will play the most significant roles in the plot development.

The dark atmosphere appropriate for the whole play has been established: an ominous atmosphere, produced by rumors of treachery, hatreds, vaunting ambition—all ready to run rampant, barely checked by royal authority. The basic tension and problem of the whole play has been suggested: will the King's rule have enough power and stability to withstand the forces threatening to undermine it, especially the force of Bolingbroke?

Act I: Scene 2

The quarrelsome tone of the first scene continues, but in a quieter way. John of Gaunt is talking in his palace to his sister-in-law the Duchess of Gloucester, the widow of the murdered Thomas. Gaunt's first words show that she has been urging him to revenge the murder of her husband. He protests that since he is Gloucester's own brother, he is even more eager than she to see justice done against the murdering butchers. But he hints that the guilt is Richard's, and only Heaven can punish the King. He adds, however, that he is confident that Heaven will, in due time, "rain hot vengeance on offenders' heads."

The Duchess is too upset to find much solace in the vague chance of divine intervention. Bitterly, she accuses Gaunt of lack of family feeling. Is his blood too old to feel the fire of brotherly affection? The former King, Edward III, had seven sons, seven vials of his blood, seven branches of his paternal root. Some have already died naturally; but Gloucester's vial has been spilt, his branch has been hacked by unnatural and murderous malice. His blood was one with Gaunt's. The same bed conceived them; the same womb molded their bodies. Gloucester's death is, in fact, Gaunt's own death. Patience in a situation like this is a poor, mean thing —and dangerous policy, too. Gaunt may be the next to be slaughtered. To safeguard his own life, he should avenge her husband's death.

> **COMMENT:** There is a nice juxtaposition here of the contrasting masculine and feminine reactions to such a stressful situation. Gaunt emphasizes the political and theoretical issues; the Duchess emphasizes the family and emotional values.

Somewhat more stern after this harangue, Gaunt replies that the quarrel is God's and that he will never approve of any attack, direct or indirect, on Richard, whom he regards as an anointed ruler, God's deputy, whose wrongdoing should be punished by God alone.

> **COMMENT:** Gaunt adheres to the doctrine of the Divine Right of Kings. This doctrine states that sovereigns inherit their right to

rule from their ancestors whom God appointed as rulers and as political representatives on earth of the Deity. According to this doctrine, rulers are not responsible to their subjects, but they *are* strictly responsible to God. Gaunt does not approve of Richard, but he will not violate the sacred office of king. It now becomes increasingly clear that the play involves not just the stability of Richard's rule but also the philosophy of the kingly office in general and the sources of its power.

To whom, then, cries the Duchess, can she complain, if Gaunt won't help. "To God," replies Gaunt, "the widow's champion and defense." The Duchess accepts this and says farewell to "old Gaunt." (By her repeated references to both Gaunt and his brother Edmund of York as being "old," the Duchess repeats a theme already introduced by Richard and also implies that Gaunt's failure to act may be partly due to the weakness of old age.) After expressing her hope that she will at least have the satisfaction of a Bolingbroke victory at Conventry, the Duchess concludes this scene with a speech in which she wallows in considerable self-pity. She hates to let Gaunt go. She will be left with her long, heavy sorrow, she says. For a moment she thinks she has no more to say; but then she calls him back to give him a message for his brother, the "old" Duke of York. Gaunt should tell him to visit her at her estate at Plashy (pronounced Pla' shee). But, no—he'll find it very lonely. She withdraws her invitation; let him not come. She'll go home to die. Weeping, she leaves. In her final speech she emphasizes the word "desolate." It tolls out not only the sadness of her personal bereavement and loneliness but also a kind of threat of universal affliction.

SUMMARY. This brief scene makes these facts clear:

1) The grievances and discontent so conspicuous in the first scene are not limited to Bolingbroke and Mowbray. They are felt by others, some of whom will be, like the Duchess, loud in their protests while others will, like Gaunt, quietly bide their time.

2) Gaunt believes in the Divine Right of Kings, a theory to which Richard also subscribes. Later events will reveal their rather different interpretations of it. For the present it is clear that Gaunt, because of his fidelity to the theory, will not take *action* against Richard.

3) Gaunt's old age is made increasingly obvious and will probably be functional soon in some plot development.

Act I: Scene 3

It is now September 17, and we move to Coventry for the judicial combat between Bolingbroke and Mowbray. There is much colorful pageantry and careful observance of protocol in this event. These ceremonies afford welcome, if temporary, relief from the foreboding events of the earlier scenes. The formalities proceed correctly. The Lord Marshal, who is in charge of the combat, ascertains that both combatants are ready and armed, awaiting only the arrival of the King to make their appearance. To the sound of trumpets, Richard enters, escorted by John of Gaunt, Bushy, Bagot, Green, and other attendants.

Mowbray appears with his herald. Richard directs the Lord Marshal to interrogate and swear in this first contestant. In response to the request of the Marshal, Mowbray states his name and titles,* and then his status here as the defendant knight challenged by Bolingbroke. He announces that he intends to prove Bolingbroke "a traitor to my God, my King, and me." He asks that Heaven defend him if he fight truly, as he intends to do.

Bolingbroke now appears, "plated in habiliments of war." The same formula of interrogation is followed with him. He repeats his charge of treason against Mowbray and, like the other man, prays for Heaven's favor if he fights fairly. The Marshal orders all spectators to stay well away from the combat field, called the "lists." Bolingbroke and then Mowbray request permission, through the Lord Marshal, to do homage to Richard. Bolingbroke says they are like two men starting a long pilgrimage. They wish to take formal and affectionate leave of their King and friends. Richard not only acquiesces but actually descends from his open-air throne to embrace first one and then the other. He says good-by to each, reminding Bolingbroke that if he is the one who is killed, Richard will mourn him as a cousin but will not be able to avenge him. Bolingbroke is blithe enough and says no one should weep for him if he is punctured by Mowbray's spear. He takes leave of his father and of his first cousin, the Duke of Aumerle (pronounced O merl'), who is the son of Edmund, Duke of York. He asks his father to pray that he will succeed in adding new luster to the name of Gaunt. Gaunt urges him to be "swift like lightening" and to hammer the helmet of Mowbray with thunderous blows. Bolingbroke calls on St. George and his own innocence to protect him. Mowbray asserts that his soul is dancing into the combat, happier than a freed captive. In fact, he goes to the fight as eagerly as to a jest. Richard reserves his final word and encouragement for Mowbray. He says he relies on the virtue and valor he sees in that knight's eyes.

Then, finally, the moment is at hand in which all these fine words will be put to the acid test. The two heralds march forth: the first to identify Bolingbroke again and to state his challenge; the second to identify Mowbray and to accept his challenge. The Marshal orders the sounding of the trumpets that will signal the commencement of the combat.

At this point of high suspense, even as the two mounted warriors wheel their horses and poise their spears, all this measured, punctilious formality

---

*This identification is necessary because the contestants ride in full armor with visors down. It was essential that each knight know for sure whom he was fighting. The armor in this period is the heavy plate armor that replaced the earlier chain mail.

is shattered by a small but significant action on the part of Richard. He throws down his "warder," a gilded staff symbolizing his authority over the proceedings. "Stay!" barks the startled Lord Marshal. Combatants and spectators alike freeze, their eyes riveted on Richard.

Relishing the melodrama of the moment, the King commands the two fighters to put aside their helmets and weapons and approach his throne. Then Richard announces that he and his Council have decided to exile both Bolingbroke and Mowbray. They do this in the interests of civil peace. They fear that the pride, envy, and ambition shown in this quarrel will plunge the country into civil war, and "fright fair peace" away from England. Bolingbroke's sentence is a ten-year exile. With a surprisingly mild "Thy will be done," Bolingbroke accepts the decree. He goes on to declare smoothly and hypocritically that he will be able to rejoice during his banishment in the fact that he will be warmed by the same sun that shines on his liege lord Richard.

> **COMMENT** Throughout the play there are frequent references and images that connect the sun, a common symbol for power and royalty, with first Richard and then Bolingbroke.

Mowbray's is a life sentence. He may never return to England. He is more disturbed and outspoken than Bolingbroke, declaring in sadness rather than in anger that he has deserved better from Richard. He grieves because in exile he will no longer be able to use his familiar English language. His tongue will be like an "unstringed" harp or other useless musical instrument. It will be a prisoner "enjailed" behind the heavy grating of teeth and lips. He is too old to learn a foreign tongue. Richard's sentence is, in effect, a speechless death for him.

> **COMMENT:** Mowbray seems to be fretting about a minor problem. But the language apparently symbolizes for him all aspects of his cherished English nationality. The theme of patriotism is strong in the play, as will be seen in the following acts.

Richard, although he has said that he reluctantly gave Mowbray so heavy a sentence, shows him no pity now, but tells him it is too late for complaining. He then summons both sentenced men before him and makes them swear on his royal sword that they will never meet, correspond, or conspire together during their banishment. They both so swear.

Bolingbroke, still trying to get the upper hand, tries to force a confession out of Mowbray. "Since thou hast far to go, bear not along / The clogging burden of a guilty soul." But Mowbray, far from admitting guilt, protests his innocence as he leaves. He halts his departure momentarily to turn back toward Bolingbroke, "But what thou art, God, thou, and I do know, / And all too soon, I fear, the King shall rue." These lines restore with emphasis the ominous tone of the first two scenes.

Richard gives his attention to his uncle and his cousin. Moved, he says, by Gaunt's grief, he reduces Bolingbroke's sentence to six years.

COMMENT: This is one of several incidents in the first half of the play in which Shakespeare makes it difficult for us to determine Richard's true motivation. Is he here moved by genuine pity and family affection? Or is he making a rather cowardly attempt to placate the House of Lancaster because he fears them? Or is this evidence of that vacillation or instability which is one of his worst personality defects?

Bolingbroke, perhaps to avoid humbling himself by thanking Richard, comments flatteringly on the power of a King who is able in one breath to cancel out four long years. Gaunt does thank the King for this reduction in punishment, but he asserts that he won't live to see his son return. Richard brushes this off with his irritating mannerism of disposing of a serious situation with a joke or pleasantry. Gaunt gravely reminds Richard that even royalty can't lengthen life. Richard can kill Gaunt, but, wealthy though he is, he could not buy one breath for the dead Gaunt. Richard, with considerable acuteness, sees that Gaunt is really shaken up by his son's sentence. So he, in turn, reminds Gaunt that Gaunt himself participated in the Council's decision to impose the sentences of exile. Gaunt admits this, but says his official action was an offense to his feelings as a father. Actually he was more harsh in judging his son than he would have been with a stranger. He blames Richard for allowing him to be betrayed into this excessive strictness. Richard does not respond to this except to say good-by to Bolingbroke and to advise Gaunt to do the same.

After the King's withdrawal, Aumerle tells Bolingbroke to write from his exile and let them know where he is staying. The Lord Marshal says he'll ride along with Bolingbroke to whatever seaport he will use for his departure. Gaunt, like a good parent, submerges his own grief and tries to cheer up Bolingbroke. He tells him six winters are not so long and urges him to look upon the exile as an opportunity for travel and new experiences. He can pretend that he has left the court of his own will—banishing it instead of it banishing him. Or he might tell himself that he has left England for a while to avoid an outbreak of the plague. At any rate, sorrow has less power to "bite" the man who resolutely keeps his chin up. Bolingbroke protests that pretending never really works. If one's hand is being burnt by fire, does it ease the pain to think of the snows on the Caucasian Mountains? No! To think of good when one is enduring evil just aggravates the suffering.

COMMENT: This speech of Bolingbroke is a good example of the imaginative richness of this play. He uses three separate images to show the futility of pretense; and each image is a double one, involving two contrasting items: fire versus snow; hunger versus feasting; chill versus warmth.

As they depart, Bolingbroke, like Mowbray before him, stresses his love of England.

COMMENT: As the play proceeds, this patriotism will become a strong theme, to the extent that in the end England herself may seem the victim of the tragedy with both Richard and Bolingbroke playing the role of villain in relation to her.

SUMMARY. In a change of pace from the rather static initial scenes, this scene forwards the action markedly.

1) It presents with considerable detail and exactness the first stages of a judicial combat. This ritual is colorful and makes very good "theater."

2) It "settles" the Bolingbroke-Mowbray dispute by recourse to the exile sentences. Despite the great attention given to it in this act, this dispute is only indirectly connected with the main line of the plot development. It will not matter much which man was telling the truth. It does matter very much, however, that Richard could not persuade them to make peace and that he decided to exile Bolingbroke at this time. It also matters that Richard is so irresponsible in allowing the preparations for the combat to proceed when he knows that there will be no combat; that he is so dramatic in his cancellation of the affair; that he is so inconsistent in his attitude toward Mowbray and in his sentencing of Bolingbroke.

3) It moves both Bolingbroke and Mowbray into their departures from England.

This scene also adds depth to our knowledge of the three chief characters.

1) Richard again settles for appearances when he allows himself to think that by banishing Mowbray and especially Bolingbroke he has actually solved the problems they present. As indicated above, it shows that Richard is capable of playing with his power as King when he waits to the last minute to cancel the combat. It also shows him as heartless in his treatment of Mowbray, who seems to have been his good friend.

2) Gaunt takes on a new and attractive dimension in his role as father. That the sturdy and, on the whole, admirable Gaunt approves of his son and supports him assures us early in the play that Bolingbroke is not really vicious. He may never be a very sympathetic character; he may act like a usurper; but we will remember that he had the love and approval of Gaunt.

3) Bolingbroke is hypocritical or at least opportunistic in his acquiescence to his sentence. More important, his nature appears to be as *unwilling* to settle for appearances and self-delusion as Richard's is so fatally *willing*.

Act I: Scene 4

King Richard is again at his court with two of his followers, Bagot and Green.* Aumerle enters, and Richard chides him rather peevishly for his

---

*Although described as servants, these two men, and also their friend Bushy, belong to the minor nobility. They have considerable authority and are closer to Richard than most of the high-born nobles.

attendance on the departing Bolingbroke. Aumerle protests that he rode only to the highway junction with Bolingbroke. Any tears that he shed at their separation were caused by the strong northeast wind blowing into his face, not by sympathy for the exile.

> **COMMENT:** Aumerle is a shifty character who at this stage, at least, is trying to ingratiate himself with both of his cousins, Richard and Bolingbroke. He is evidently shrewd enough to see that Richard's power may in the future be challenged by Bolingbroke. He is not, however, very energetic in any of his maneuvers.

Seeing that the King is suspicious of him, Aumerle tries even harder to clear himself. He explains that he didn't answer to Bolingbroke's final "farewell"; he pretended to be too choked up with sorrow at the parting to get a word out. This trick, says Aumerle, was to avoid wishing Bolingbroke the good luck that "fare well" would mean. However, if the word "farewell" could have extended Bolingbroke's exile, Aumerle would have been glad to shout it repeatedly after the departing figure of Bolingbroke. Richard ignores this foolish exaggeration, but his mind does linger for a moment on what *will* happen when Bolingbroke's comparatively brief exile is over. He tells Aumerle that this cousin of theirs probably will not consider them his friends.

Richard then comments sourly on the throng that watched Bolingbroke's departure and on Bolingbroke's irritating playing-up to them. This is a vivid passage that takes you right into a medieval working-class crowd lining the roadway to see a popular hero. Bolingbroke is the hero, and he has the true politician's touch and charm. He smiles at them as a group. But, better than that, he makes them feel he is aware of them as individuals. He takes off his cap with a flourish to a girl who sells oysters, and he makes a deep bow to two carters who call him a greeting. In a master stroke he wins both their admiration and their sympathy by convincing them that under his cheery manner his heart is broken by the banishment sentence. No wonder Richard's teeth are on edge as he describes this scene and comments at the end that Bolingbroke acted as if he were the acknowledged heir to the throne.

> **COMMENT:** In this and his other two speeches in this scene, Richard reveals weaknesses in his character that are perhaps more serious than the ineffectualness he has already displayed. These weaknesses are:
>
> 1) A contemptuous attitude toward the common people.
>
> 2) An admission of too lavish expenditures in maintaining his court.
>
> 3) Unwise fiscal policy of "farming" his realm, that is selling to certain individuals the privilege of collecting and keeping tax revenues.

> 4) A willingness to resort to unscrupulous extortion of money from his wealthy subjects.
>
> 5) A calloused flippancy that allows him to hope for Gaunt's early death so that he can seize the Lancaster possessions.
>
> In addition, he continues his unrealistic and silly self-delusion that, because he has gone into exile, Bolingbroke is no longer a threat. He knows better than that, as he occasionally shows, but his nature does not let him worry much about the future.

In response to a reminder from Green, Richard announces that they must now depart for Ireland to subdue the rebellion there. (The English claim to sovereignty over Ireland dated from the twelfth century, but rebellions recurrently challenged that claim.) Suddenly Bushy enters. He brings word of John of Gaunt's serious illness. Richard immediately sees advantage for himself in this and frankly hopes for Gaunt's quick death. He indicates that he will delay his departure to the Irish wars to visit Gaunt at Ely House. With the revoltingly insensitive "Pray God we may make haste, and come too late" (that is, too late to find Gaunt alive), Richard leads his retinue off stage.

> **COMMENT:** Ely (pronounced Ee'lee) House was a London town house that Gaunt had borrowed temporarily from the Bishop of Ely. Part of it still stands and is one of modern London's treasured survivals of the medieval period.

SUMMARY. This is a short scene, but it does contribute a number of important points.

1) That Bolingbroke has gone into exile, escorted for a distance by Aumerle (and probably other nobles), and applauded along the way by the populace.

2) That Bolingbroke was pleased by this applause and tried to stimulate even more affection for himself among the common people.

3) That Richard is on the eve of a military expedition to Ireland, an expedition that will require much money to finance.

4) That Richard intends to raise the money, even if he has to use methods that his subjects will rightly protest.

5) That Gaunt is grievously sick, and that Richard is glad that he is.

6) That Richard's complex character includes certain unattractive features, some of them very dangerous to him and to England. He can be fickle, jealous, snobbish, scheming, and heartless.

It is now becoming clear that this is a play in which it is difficult to find a hero. At this point Richard, although he seems to be the main character, is rapidly disqualifying himself by both his weakness as a ruler and his personal faults. Bolingbroke is a possibility, but we need to know more about him.

Act II: Scene 1

We are now in Ely House in London. Gaunt, sick and weakened, awaits with his brother Edmund, Duke of York (usually referred to as "York"), the visit of the King. Gaunt's first words reveal that he intends to tell the King flatly how wrong and dangerous some of his policies are. York, although he shares his brother's opinion that Richard is a weak, unsteady, and willful King, advises Gaunt to save his breath "for all in vain comes counsel to his ear."

> **COMMENT:** One of the minor but clever accomplishments of this scene is the revelation of the difference between the personalities of these two elderly brothers. They are basically in accord, but Gaunt is stern and reproving while York is timid and acquiescent.

Gaunt says that the words of a dying man should have a special force and should "undeaf" Richard's ear. Small chance, believes York. In his opinion, the kingly ear is far too busy listening to flattery, to the latest popular poetry, and to fashion reports from Italy. This reminder of Richard's frivolous and expensive interests serves only to stiffen Gaunt's determination and to rouse him to one of the most famous speeches of the play. In this speech he praises England, "this other Eden, ... this precious stone set in the silver sea, ... this dear, dear land." He praises her for her power and majesty, for her military might ("seat of Mars"), for her closeness to perfection (a "demi-Paradise"), for the fortunate sea-protected position, for her royalty ("feared" and "famous") who have traditionally been true to Christian and chivalric ideals.

> **COMMENT:** This speech and Gaunt's dying concern for England are major contributions to the fervent patriotism of the play. The speech itself is one of the finest literary tributes ever paid to England.

And "this blessed plot" is now, because of Richard's shaky financial arrangements, bound in by "inky blots and rotten parchment bonds." England is virtually enslaved by his questionable money deals. They hear the approach of the King, and hastily York urges Gaunt to be mild and to avoid antagonizing Richard.

The King is accompanied by his Queen, various courtiers, and attendants. Gently the Queen inquires for Gaunt's health; but before she can be answered, Richard asks brusquely, "How is't with aged Gaunt?" Again the dig, the gratuitous insistence on Gaunt's age. Gaunt picks up the cue for the pun and plays on the meanings of the word "gaunt" with a virtuosity that makes us echo Richard's "Can sick men play so nicely with their names?"

> **COMMENT:** The verbal facility is, of course, Shakespeare's (and, it must be admitted, he's the fellow who is showing off a bit here). It is one of the major stylistic characteristics of the play. Like most of Shakespeare's earlier plays, this drama is marked by rich, sometimes undisciplined inventiveness in description, imagery, and wordplay.

Gaunt's point, however, stands out clear enough from all the luxuriance of the language. Richard's misgovernment of England has made Gaunt gaunt with worry. Richard, too, is on the point of death—political death, because of his financial policies. If his grandfather, King Edward III, could have foreseen the nature of Richard's rule, he would never have agreed to Richard's succession.

This stings Richard to threaten Gaunt with execution. Only their close relationship saves him, says the King. Even that did not protect Gloucester, retorts Gaunt. But now the dying man has no more strength and no more desire for talk. He orders his servants to bear him to bed—and then to his grave. After he leaves, York tries briefly and to no avail to assure Richard of the loyalty of the Lancasters (Gaunt and Bolingbroke). They are interrupted by the Earl of Northumberland's report that Gaunt will speak no more; "his tongue is now a stringless instrument"; he is dead.

So much for that, says Richard in effect. Then he announces that he is seizing "the plate, coin, revenues and movables" of Gaunt to finance his Irish expedition.

> **COMMENT:** This one rather brief speech shows Richard at his worst: calloused in his treatment of Gaunt's death; incredibly arbitrary, foolhardy, and short-sighted in his appropriation of the Lancaster property.

York objects on three scores. Such wrongdoing is a disgrace to Richard's upbringing; his father, the Black Prince, would never have sunk so low. It is completely unjust to Bolingbroke, the heir to the Lancaster properties. It is extremely dangerous to Richard himself. Richard ignores York's advice (as does almost everyone that York attempts to advise), says he's off to Ireland on the morrow, and appoints York his deputy or representative in his absence. Then he departs. With him go the Queen and most of the courtiers. Three noblemen linger, however. They are the Earl of Northumberland, Lord Ross, and Lord Willoughby.

> **COMMENT:** These are all powerful magnates. The Earl of Northumberland is the head of the strongest family in the north of England, the Percy family. So influential is the Percy name in the North that, should he so command, that part of England would rise almost to a man, even in rebellion against the reigning king. The title "earl" indicate a very high nobleman. Ordinarily only royalty itself and dukes outranked earls.

After some preliminary sparring to feel out their individual opinions, they find that they are agreed in strong opposition to the King. They have long resented the burdensome taxation, and now they see an additional threat in the injustice to Bolingbroke. If the King can do this to Bolingbroke who is a member of the royal family and the strongest nobleman at court, what defense would they in their less protected positions have against him? Northumberland then confides to them the startling news that Bolingbroke is returning from exile, accompanied by several important noblemen. They have, in fact, already sailed from Brittany in "eight tall ships," well manned and equipped. They are to land at Ravenspurgh (pronounced Ray'ven sperg) in Yorkshire, far to the north of London. With Bolingbroke back, Northumberland hints, the days of real kingship may return. His excited invitation to the other two to join him in a speedy trip north to the Channel port where Richard is to land is enthusiastically accepted. They hasten away to mount their horses for the long ride.

SUMMARY. This very important scene underlines the contrast between appearance and reality. The value of recognizing this contrast is one of the play's main observations about life. The scene accomplishes this by making the following points about the King:

1) Richard believes that Gaunt's death has relieved him of a threat. In reality, this uncle's death deprives him of sound advice, particularly about financial matters. The treachery of the three noblemen at the end of the scene springs chiefly from their dissatisfaction with Richard's policies about money.

2) Richard believes that Bolingbroke in exile can do nothing about the Crown's seizure of the Lancaster holdings. In reality, this very act of seizure will win for Bolingbroke many adherents who object to Richard's harsh treatment of his cousin.

3) Richard believes that he is quite secure in leaving England for the Irish campaign. In reality, he leaves at home a seditious conspiracy far more dangerous to him than the rebellion in Ireland.

4) Richard accepts at face value the pretense of loyalty shown him by Northumberland, Ross, and Willoughby. He should have guessed what a shattering effect his appropriation of the vast Lancaster property would have on other nobles, as well as on Bolingbroke. But Richard is both a poor judge of other people's reactions and also temperamentally too impatient to try to discover what really lies beneath the conventional, painted smiles on his courtiers' faces.

Act II: Scene 2

In the interval between this and the first scene of the act, Richard departs for Ireland.

In effective contrast to the excitement and rush at the end of the previous scene, this scene opens on a subdued, sad note. The mood is set by the

Queen who talks with Bushy and Bagot at the royal palace of Windsor (a short distance up the Thames from London). She is in low spirits. Her sadness is explained in part, of course, by the departure of her "sweet Richard." But she is also deeply disturbed by a vague, nameless fear. Bushy tries to persuade her that it is just that she is lonesome for Richard. "It may be so," she admits "but yet my inward soul / Persuades me it is otherwise .... / I cannot but be sad, so heavy sad." She does not have to wait long for the vindication of her feminine premonitions.

First, Green enters with the "hope" that Richard has not yet left for Ireland, as we, however, know full well he has.

> **COMMENT:** Note the word-play here with the word "hope." Elizabethan audiences apparently enjoyed this type of exchange even at such moments of high and serious suspense.

The word has come that Bolingbroke has landed at Ravenspurgh. The three conspirators of the previous scene have joined him, as have also a Lord Beaumond, and two of the Earl of Northumberland's relatives. These relatives are his son Henry (Harry) Percy, and his brother the Earl of Worcester (pronounced: Woos' ter). The last named was an official in Richard's court, but broke his staff of office and defected. All have been proclaimed traitors, but to subdue the revolt an energetic and firm leader is required. In ironic contrast to that emphatic need, the King's deputy, the aged York, enters, too old, as he laments, to support himself, let alone underprop all England. He confirms the report Green has given, and, in a distraught fashion, tries to attend all at once to the demands of the emergency—summoning any nobles still loyal (most have fled, he says, and the common people are uninterested), mustering forces, raising money, notifying the King, attending to the shocked Queen. His intentions are good, but he is unable to execute them in any effective way. Also, he is deprived of two supports that he counted on: His son, Aumerle, has disappeared; and, in the midst of the flurry, he hears that the Duchess of Gloucester is dead. Eventually he mentions the problem that is probably more responsible for his confusion than any debility of old age: "Both are my kinsmen. / The one is my sovereign, whom both my oath / And my duty bids defend. The other again / Is my kinsman, whom the King hath wronged, / Whom conscience and my kindred bids to right."

> **COMMENT:** Again we find Shakespeare warming and humanizing the political situation. He is aware that many viewers will find it hard to relate to or perhaps even really understand the politics in the play. To hold the interest of his audience, he coalesces with the political struggle the tensions of family relationships that all of us have experienced and for which we have quick, ready sympathy.

York orders Bushy and the others to assemble soldiers and meet him at Berkeley (pronounced Bark' lee) Castle in western England. He deplores the fact that he has no time to go to pay his last respects to the dead

Duchess of Gloucester. Then the old man fussily leads out the Queen, to "dispose" of her, as he rather tactlessly puts it.

Bushy, Bagot, and Green remin behind. They very gloomily assess their personal prospects, as well as the national distress. Bushy has learned that the winds on the Irish Channel will favor the ship bringing Richard the bad news, but will delay the ship which should return him to England. He is pessimistic about the chances of raising an army large enough to stop Bolingbroke. They all agree that the populace is antagonistic to Richard because of the tax burdens. They themselves, as well-known confidants of the King, are very vulnerable. They pay no attention to York's final order to them. Bushy and Green resolve to go west to Bristol Castle to join the loyal Earl of Wiltshire. Bagot, however, decides to take off for Ireland. He hopes to join Richard before Richard embarks for the return to England. They bid each other farewell. Bagot and Green are fatalistically sure that it is for the last time. They have no confidence in York, the "poor Duke."

SUMMARY. Although he does not appear in it, this scene is very much concerned with the King. Indirectly, it shows his incompetence as an administrator. We are appalled by the feebleness of the control group to whom Richard entrusted the welfare of England in his absence.

1) Officially York represents the King. He is both unwilling and unable to cope with the revolt. He "knows not what to do." He even wishes he had had his head cut off at the time the ax fell on Gloucester—although, of course, he would not like to commit treason, even for so fine a reward as decapitation—a conscientious second-thought, amusingly typical of the cautious York.

2) The Queen, although sensitive and loyal, is not capable of taking control either in her own person or as a power behind York.

3) Other court officials, represented especially by Worcester, are so shaky in their fealty to Richard that they desert their posts at first word of the revolt.

4) Bushy, Bagot, and Green, instead of trying to use constructively whatever official power they may have, devote all their energy to saving their own skins.

In these inadequacies and failures of his representatives Richard's lack of true kingship is all too apparent. Apparent also, but not stated in so many words, is the growing danger to England in this situation. John of Gaunt's praise of her has just made England seem especially precious. Therefore, this exposing of her to the ravages of civil rebellion appears all the more blameworthy. This juxtaposition is a good example of Shakespeare's careful planning, even to small details.

Act II: Scene 3

This scene proves that the reports that so alarmed Richard's followers in the last scene were by no means exaggerated. It also provides a good mood relief in its contrasting optimism and vigor. It satisfies, too, our curiosity about the activities of the rebels. We find Bolingbroke leading some forces through a wild countryside in Gloucestershire (pronounced Glos' ter sheer). He is accompanied by Northumberland. They have marched southwestward across central England from the English Channel port where Bolingbroke had landed. Bolingbroke asks wearily how far they are from their destination, which turns out to be the same Berkeley Castle that York mentioned in the previous scene. Northumberland says that he doesn't know. It's all strange territory to him. Its very roughness makes the miles seem longer, but he counts himself lucky to have had the pleasant company of Bolingbroke to shorten the way. Northumberland's son, Harry Percy, enters and reports that his uncle, the Earl of Worcester, has deserted the court of Richard to ally himself with Bolingbroke. Worcester had sent his nephew to spy out York's strength at Berkeley.

The young man's father then introduces him to Bolingbroke, and the youth promises the rebel his service, which he says will become more valuable as he grows to manhood.

> **COMMENT:** This is a richly ironic foreshadowing of events in the sequel play *Henry IV, Part 1*. In that play the Percys break with Bolingbroke, who has become King Henry IV. The same Harry Percy will then be the famous Hotspur who fights a good but losing fight against Prince Hal, the son of Bolingbroke.

Young Harry gives them the good news that Berkeley Castle is actually within sight. He tells them also that it is held by York and Lord Berkeley, and just then the Lords Ross and Willoughby join the group. Immediately afterward Lord Berkeley and then York himself appear.

Bolingbroke salutes York with "My noble uncle" and kneels before him. But York is for the moment proof against such flattery. "Grace me no grace, nor uncle me no uncle," he says testily. Bolingbroke may be his nephew, but he is also a detestable traitor who has alarmed his country and defied his king in the person of his deputy.

> **COMMENT:** This is one of York's best speeches. In it rings again the love of England and the devotion to the anointed, divinely ordained King. For once, he throws caution to the winds and says what he *really* thinks.

Bolingbroke pleads the special injustice to him of Richard's seizure of his possessions. If York had died first, Gaunt would have aided Aumerle, York's son. York does not deny that Bolingbroke had plenty of provocation, but he insists that Bolingbroke's armed rebellion is wrong. But with that bit of plain, forthright speaking, the old man's fire is suddenly spent.

He announces his intention of remaining neutral since he does not have power to sudue the rebels. He even offers them the hospitality of Berkeley Castle. Bolingbroke accepts the offer and says he hopes to persuade York to advance with them on Bristol Castle to crush Bushy and Bagot. (It is these two whom he mentions. Actually Bushy and Green are at Bristol. Bagot, as we know, intended to make for Ireland.)

> **COMMENT:** Bolingbroke's skill is seen here, not so much in the capitulation of the enfeebled York (which cannot be credited directly to Bolingbroke), as in his immediate move to consolidate and forward his gains by drawing York from a neutral position into the campaign against Bushy and Green.

York is now frankly out of his depth. "Things past redress are now with me past care." But he clings to a small foothold of independence. Bolingbroke has to be satisfied with "It may be I'll go with you. But yet I'll pause, / For I am loath to break our country's laws."

SUMMARY. In this scene we watch more unfolding of the character of Bolingbroke. In a kind of contrapuntal movement his character development will balance the exposition of the character of Richard. By the force of his character, Bolingbroke's fortunes will ascend; at the same steady rate, Richard's fortunes, by virtue of his qualities, will descend. To what we learned about Bolingbroke in Act 1, we can now add these facts:

1) He has ability to attract powerful followers, such as the Percy clan; he knows how to make them feel valued and eager to be in his presence.

2) He has ability to curb his emotions under criticism. In such a situation, he can give his energy to framing a calm, plausible statement in his own defense. It would have been easy for Bolingbroke to quarrel with York, to take offense at his uncle's criticism. Instead, he bridles his tongue, and answers placidly and respectfully. He senses the tired old man's need for firm, strong help, and his manner suggests that help can be found in him. Unlike Richard, Bolingbroke is a good judge of human nature.

3) He has ability to modify his strategy and to take shrewd advantage of every chance incident in his favor. A self-declared neutral York should be lured into the Bolingbroke camp. How better than by suggesting he join the attack, not against Richard or loyal nobility, but against a group of upstarts like Bushy and Green. York considers these men a bad influence on Richard, anyway.

Although perhaps no more admirable than Richard by virtue of these traits, Bolingbroke is certainly, because of them, better qualified to rule. He begins to have something of the stature of a hero, but in the political sense only. He may have the reader's or viewer's *vote;* he doesn't, yet at least, command his *heart.*

Act II: Scene 4

This very short scene adds still another item to the catalog of catastrophe that is accumulating for Richard. The action takes place in a military encampment in Wales. In an abrupt farewell speech, the Captain of a Welsh fighting force informs the Earl of Salisbury, a nobleman still loyal to Richard, that his troops are departing. They have waited ten days beyond the appointed date for the King, and still he has not appeared. Salisbury's reply is very brief and mechanical, as if he were drained of hope. He does ask the Captain to remain another day, for in this Welsh force "the King reposeth all his confidence."

> **COMMENT:** As we learn later, if they had waited that extra day, they would have effected their rendezvous with Richard. With that force behind him, the King's attitude to Bolingbroke might have been quite different. However, this is to be a tragedy of character. Eventually Richard was bound to meet his downfall.

In contrast to Salisbury's emotional flatness and lack of conviction, the Captain's firm reiteration of the Welsh intention is colorful and charged with assurance. His men will leave because they are sure Richard is dead. They have "evidence" in the form of Welsh trees unnaturally withered, a bloody hue observed on the moon, sinister warnings from lean prophets, and other omens of disaster. So, fortified with "reasons," the Welsh Captain stalks off.

Salisbury, alone for his final speech, laments the decline of Richard's fortunes with a much freer flow of language than he could muster to talk of Richard's plans. He associates Richard with the setting sun. It is a bad weather sun, a weeping sun foreseeing "storms to come."

> **COMMENT:** "Weeping sun" is, of course, a bold image, but it does reinforce very effectively the idea of disaster in the symbol setting sun. It also provides another example, especially noteworthy since it appears in the last lines of the act, of the use of the sun symbol in relation to Richard. But now the opposing element of water is introduced. These two elements will continue to be significant in the symbolism that illuminates Richard's condition.

In his final lines, Salisbury speaks of the defections to Bolingbroke and of the general worsening of Richard's fortunes.

SUMMARY. Although a brief two dozen lines in length and entrusted to two very minor characters, this scene is most effective. It serves as a culmination of the events that precede and as a transition to the great third act. It gives factual information of importance to the plot's progress.

1) Richard's return from Ireland is expected but has been delayed.

2) He is evidently expected to land somewhere along the Welsh coast.

3) His resources are now so diminished that he must place "all his confidence" in a troop of uninterested Welsh soldiers.

4) His erstwhile friends continue to desert to Bolingbroke.

5) His supporters, if Salisbury is typical, are discouraged.

This scene's function is not limited to factual information. In addition:

1) It throws over this information the sinister shadow of the various omens cited by the Welsh Captain. Even those who recognize these omens for what they are, rank superstitions, will respond to their emotional and imaginative suggestiveness. Since these omens involve mysterious, supernatural forces, they seem to enlarge the arena of Richard's struggle and so make it the more awesome.

2) It stirs our first feelings of real pity for Richard. He seems fated for a ruin so catastrophic that we feel sorry for him, even though, so far, we have found little attractive in his character. Of course, Bolingbroke's similar lack of endearing characteristics makes easier the slight stirrings of sympathy for Richard.

Act III: Scene 1

Bolingbroke, York, Northumberland, Ross, Percy, and Willoughby all troop onto the stage. Soldiers also lead in Bushy and Green, fettered, obviously prisoners. In the background looms Bristol Castle which the unfortunate Bushy and Green had sought as a refuge. It has, however, fallen to Bolingbroke, and their doom is sealed. This Bolingbroke makes clear immediately. He says he must rehearse their crimes to justify his execution of them, but he will not stress their sins since that could be disturbing to men so soon to die. He does not want to be guilty of that kind of offense against charity.

> **COMMENT:** Bolingbroke's concern for their souls' welfare, his concern that they should not be plunged into the dark sin of despair, may well be sincere. Religious attitudes of this type are almost as common in Renaissance as in medieval literature.

His general accusation is that they have been an evil influence on the King. Then he states rapidly the particulars of his case against them.

1) They have established an unnatural relationship with Richard which has alienated the King and Queen.

> **COMMENT:** This reference to homosexual practices seems a loose thread in the plot. It may go back to some source Shakespeare used rather carelessly and incompletely. At any rate, it is hard to reconcile the charge with what other scenes show us of the relationship between Richard and the Queen.

2) They have "misinterpreted" Bolingbroke to the King and so caused Bolingbroke's exile.

3) During his exile they grabbed as many of his possessions as they could. He could, he says, double the list but this is sufficient to warrant their condemnation. He orders their immediate execution.

> **COMMENT:** Note that Bolingbroke's emphasis is on Bushy and Green's offenses against *him* rather than on their disservice to the kingdom. We keep waiting for some personally attractive qualities in Bolingbroke to make us really confident that the change of power from Richard to Bolingbroke, a change that seems certain now, will actually be a marked improvement. So far, despite Bolingbroke's obvious political superiority, we have little to reassure us about him personally.

Each condemned man indicates, whether in bravado or in sincerity (it is difficult to tell for the speeches are very brief), that Bolingbroke is evil and unjust. Each affirms that he goes with a calm mind to his death. They are led out to execution by Northumberland.

Bolingbroke takes a minute to ask York to give the Queen, who is sheltered in York's house, a message of regard and commendation. With that the energetic Bolingbroke summons away the other lords "to fight with Glendower and his complices."

> **COMMENT:** This reference to Glendower (pronounced Glen do er) is another loose thread in the plot. There is no other earlier or later reference in this play to conflict with this man. Owen Glendower was an historical person who lived in the late 1300's and early 1400's. He was a leader of Welsh revolts against English rule and an especially daring guerrilla fighter. Among his Welsh followers, he had a reputation as a great magician and conjurer. He does figure quite prominently in Shakespeare's *Henry IV, Part 1*. He is an ally of the Percies in their revolt against King Henry.

SUMMARY. The chief service of this short scene is to impress us with the steady advance of Bolingbroke's assumption of power.

1) He has now penetrated, without effective opposition, to the western shores of England.

2) He has captured an important loyalist stronghold, Bristol Castle.

3) He has seized and executed two of Richard's intimates. Although the execution is not preceded by even the pretense of a trial. Bolingbroke's statement of his grievances has a kind of law court formality. But despite this very slight concession to justice, Bolingbroke's handling of the affair seems self-centered and high-handed, partly an act of personal vengeance. Yet, whatever his motives, he has been able to accomplish this act which is so very hostile to Richard.

4) His message to the Queen is kindly enough, but it is another way of telling us that he is rapidly becoming the power in the land, the power to whom even the Queen must look for protection.

5) He is sure enough of his power to contemplate a type of foreign war. And in that war he seems to be assuming the rank of commander-in-chief of the English forces.

Act III: Scene 2

Again we have a castle scene, and again the locale is western England. We are on the Welsh coast. Nearby is Barkloughly (pronounced Bar klaw' klee) Castle, a fortress as stark and grim as Bristol Castle. But this time our eyes and ears have some diversion. Drums beat a royal flourish, and there is a show of flags and standards. Richard has finally made it to England. He is accompanied in his entrance by the Bishop of Carlisle,* Aumerle, and a small detachment of soldiers. Apparently he has had a rough as well as slow crossing of the Irish Channel. The King's ship has been "tossing" on "breaking seas," according to Aumerle. (We never discover just where Aumerle joined the King, but presumably it was at the Welsh port where Richard landed.)

But for more reasons than the difficulty of the sea voyage, Richard is very, very happy to be once again on his native English soil. (Again the theme of patriotism, of love of England, is stressed.) He addresses that dear native earth, and he bends to salute it with a caress of his hand. Like a child after a separation from its mother, he says he both weeps and smiles to be restored to the security of his own land. He weeps because of the hardships of the separation, and smiles because those hardships are now no more. Like a child, he immediately has a petition. He asks that fostering English earth to do what it can to thwart Bolingbroke. It should withhold from the rebel forces its pleasant scents and sights, and instead annoy their marching feet with venomous spiders, toads, and stinging nettles. He suggests that it hide a poisonous adder (the only poisonous snake native to England) in every flower they stoop to pick. Conscious of his followers' stares and perhaps grins at the strangeness of this address to the insensible earth, Richard tells them not to mock him. This very earth and its stones would indeed rise in defence of any rebellion against their true King. Carlisle agrees that the Divine Right of Kings will operate to help Richard, but emphasizes that Heaven helps him who helps himself, that Heaven expects him to take advantage of every means to maintain his rule. Aumerle eagerly seconds Carlisle, pointing out that they have been at fault in letting Bolingbroke make so many uncontested advances.

*The high churchmen, such as bishops, of medieval England were often large landowners and practiced politicians. They also were lords of the realm and ranked with the higher nobility. As such they could be deeply involved in many political and even, in a noncombatant fashion, military actions.

Richard is moved to one of his most poetic speeches. Doesn't his cousin Aumerle know that it is when the sun is absent from our world and night descends that wrongdoers lurk and flourish? But when the sun returns, its rays search out all the dark corners to expose and shame the criminals. So Bolingbroke, "this thief, this traitor," has been making the most of Richard's absence and of England's resulting darkness to hatch his wicked schemes. But with Richard's return, like the sun's eastern rising after its "trip" through the regions on the other side of the globe, light begins again to flood England. Bolingbroke himself will be shamed by the exposure of his infamy. The language of this speech up to this point is very flowery and very confident. Richard now moves on to the reason for his confidence. It is the theory we already know to be basic to his political philosophy. "Not all the water in the rough rude sea / Can wash the balm [consecrated oil used in coronation ceremony] off from the anointed king. / The breath of worldly men cannot depose / The deputy elected by the Lord."

> **COMMENT:** The first metaphor here is one of the two opposing images that Shakespeare throughout the play associates with the kingly character. The favorable image is that of fire (often in the form of the sun as in the first part of this same speech), and the unfavorable image is that of water. This water image suggests a threat, but at this point no more than that, to the King.

Richard's final lines show how very high above the practicalities of the situation his confidence in his divine right to rule has floated him. For every rebel Bolingbroke raises, God, he declares, has an angel to fight for "His Richard." And as his imagination plays with that fascinating picture of opposing ranks of men and angels in battle array, he arrives at the conclusion that is so obvious to him, and so comforting—if angels fight men, the issue can only be victory for the angelic hosts.

> **COMMENT:** This self-delusion is very close to madness. But Richard is not mad.
>
> 1) He has a hyperactive imagination that easily invents fantasies.
>
> 2) He has the kind of mind that allows itself to be satisfied with such fantasies instead of solid and real fact.
>
> 3) He has the kind of conscience that prefers to slip away from responsibilities by pretending the responsibilities don't exist or will be discharged by someone else. So here he finds much satisfaction in his fantasy of angel help. He knows it is a gross exaggeration of what the Divine Right theory promises a monarch. But he cherishes as long as he can the pleasing dream which excuses him from effort. These personality traits combine here with his very real and sincere belief that he is a divinely chosen or elected king. Together they account for his strange words and actions in this scene—words and actions that are bizarre but not irrational.

Richard is now, of course, at a peak of his confidence—invincible angel hosts fight for him. Watch the terrible swiftness with which he is plummeted down from this emotional height.

Richard interrupts himself as Salisbury, who, we know, is one of the few lords still loyal to him, enters. "How far lies your power?" inquires Richard. Despite his fantasies, he realizes he must attend to some practical issues. He wants to know the location of the Welsh force that Salisbury was responsible for contacting. "Nor near nor farther off, my gracious lord, / than this weak arm," puns Salisbury wryly. Actually, he now commands no other power than the might of his own muscle. He tells Richard of the shift of the Welsh troops, twelve thousand fighting men strong, to the side of Bolingbroke. By one brief day Richard missed the rendezvous that would have convinced them that their omen lied and their king still lived. Small wonder that Salisbury warned Richard that he brought a message of despair. Richard pales. When Aumerle comments on this change, Richard says he has good reason to be pale. The blood of thousands of fighting men has been drained from his cheeks. He expects to continue to look pale—and dead—as his supporters defect.

Aumerle tries to prevent this despondent reaction, and Richard does attempt to recover his spirits. Is he not a King? Isn't his very name a power? What if a "puny subject" strikes out at him? Who can really harm majesty on its heights? And anyway York has plenty of troops.

Another lord loyal to Richard, Sir Stephen Scroop, strides in. He *wishes* his king happiness, but says he can *bring* him none. Hearing this, Richard again changes his attitude. He says he is prepared now for the worst. Has he lost his kingdom? So what—it was a heavy care. Is Bolingbroke trying to be his equal? Well, they'll serve God together, and so be fellows. Do his people rebel? He can't prevent it; let them defy God, if they dare. Let Scroop cry whatever calamity he likes; the worst is death, and death is bound to come some time. Scroop says it is well the King is so philosophical. A mighty flood is moving over England, the flood of the revolt loosed on the land by Bolingbroke.

> **COMMENT:** The water image identified with Bolingbroke is moving to oppose the fire (sun) image of Richard.

People of all ages and conditions are joining the rebel ranks. Old men, boys, clerics, and even women choose unaccustomed weapons and join the regular soldiers.

Richard inquires with rising anger for Bagot, Bushy, Green, and the Earl of Wiltshire. Why did they let Bolingbroke get such a start? They'll pay for their failure to do their duty. "I warrant they have made peace with Bolingbroke." Scroop, a little nettled by Richard's failure to appreciate the difficulties of those who were on the home front, says that they have indeed done just that. Richard flies into a real rage. They are villains, vipers, turncoats, dogs, snakes. Still the stream of verbal attacks flows. They are triple-dyed Judases. "Terrible Hell make war / Upon their spotted souls!"

Dryly, Scroop suggests that Richard "uncurse their souls." These men have lost their lives in fidelity to Richard and lie now in their graves. All at Bristol Castle met this fate.

> **COMMENT:** There is some confusion about Bagot. He was the one who decided to go to Ireland when Bushy and Green selected Bristol Castle as a haven. Apparently he didn't make connection with Richard. In this scene he is mentioned again with Bushy and Green, but he is not actually named as one of those executed at Bristol. Either Shakespeare wants to suggest that this present group has no definite information about him, or else Shakespeare himself had lost track of this minor thread in his plot. We do hear more of Bagot later.

Aumerle inquires for his father and the army they think York must be leading. This is apparently to give Richard something more encouraging to think about. Richard interprets it that way, anyway. But Richard is now as low and depressed as he was exhilarated before the arrival of Salisbury. Let no man speak to him of comfort. "Let's talk of graves, of worms, of epitaphs." And he does just that, at some length but with great effectiveness. This is one of the most famous speeches of the play. His words are rather morbid, and he is again playing a role suggested by his imagination. But he does, nevertheless, stir us with his reflections on the transientness and hollowness of earthly glory. They and their possessions are in the hands of Bolingbroke. Nothing of their own can they claim, except their bodies. They can pass the time telling "sad stories of the death of Kings"—usually assassinations. Within the very "hollow crown" of monarchy Death grins and mocks, and at the appointed moment strikes. And he? Well, after all he is only flesh and blood like themselves, subject to the same afflictions. Indeed, he is a *subject* and no king. Let them no longer reverence him.

Carlisle can stand no more of this reaction which seems maudlin self-pity to him. He urges Richard to buck up. He is a worse enemy to himself than is Bolingbroke; let him make some plans. After all, in such a situation to fight and die is better than not to fight at all. Changeable as a weathercock and as responsive to influence, Richard *is* stimulated by Carlisle, and turns again to Scroop for the report on York.

But the unfortunate Scroop has to admit that he plays "the torturer by small and small." His last and worst message is "Your uncle York is joined with Bolingbroke, / And all your northern castles yielded up, / And all your southern gentlemen in arms / Upon his party." "Thou hast said enough!" is Richard's sober acknowledgement of this report. Although momentarily shocked into that sober brevity, Richard again speaks emotionally as he leaves. He says they had been wrong in trying to raise his spirits. He now will yield himself completely to despair, pining away in Flint Castle. He gives orders for his followers to be discharged. Let them go join Bolingbroke's dawning day. Richard's sun sinks under night's blackness.

SUMMARY. This very important and very clever scene is a masterly revelation of aspects of Richard's character not emphasized so far.

1) One aspect is the great changeability of both his moods and convictions—his constitutional lack of stability. With almost the regularity of a pendulum, he alternates throughout the scene between exhilaration and despondency.

a. He enters delighted to be back in England and certain that the very earth of England will act to stop rebellion. The slight objection of Carlisle and Aumerle to such extravagant optimism he brushes aside. He indulges happily his Walter Mitty-like dream of the ease with which Bolingbroke will be disposed of, as soon as Richard's sun-like power shines again on the land, a power that will be backed by legions of God's angels.

b. But Salisbury brings word of the Welsh desertion. Richard collapses into despondency.

c. Prodded by Aumerle, he quickly rebounds, to insist that his kingly majesty can not be harmed.

d. But Scroop reports the growth of the rebellion and the executions at Bristol. Richard immediately leaps to the conclusion that he is no longer a king.

e. Again, just faint encouragement from Carlisle and Aumerle restores him to his throne and makes him loudly defiant of Bolingbroke.

f. But Scroop goes on to report the full extent of the rebellion, and Richard is ready to give Bolingbroke the victory without a struggle.

Critics disagree in their attempts to explain the reason for Richard's changeableness. It may be that he veered around so easily because he had no personal stability in his position as King. He probably was not monarch material and didn't have either the ability or the inclination to rule in the full political sense. His vacillation in this scene is accentuated by the steadiness and reasonableness of Carlisle and the attendant laymen.

2) Another aspect is his extreme talkativeness. He does most of the talking in the scene. One of the subtle points that very inconspicuously enriches the style of the scene is the contrast between Richard's long speeches and the comparatively brief comments of the others. There are at least two facts worth noticing about his talkativeness.

a. He speaks very well, fluently and vividly, holding our interest. This linguistic fluency is one reason that some critics think that Shakespeare decided, rightly or wrongly, that the historical Richard was an artist at heart, with the gifts of a poet and perhaps of an actor. Shakespeare may have been saying that Richard's tragedy was that he had to stifle his real genius to try to be a king, a job for which he probably had no ability.

b. This talkativeness is terribly ironic at this point because he should have been acting. All the energy that he needs for conducting his campaign against Bolingbroke he wastes here in protracted talk and emotional blow-ups.

Richard is weary at the scene's end. And we are too, for we are worn down by our effort to keep pace with his mood changes. But we know King Richard better. What we learn of him from this scene probably does not make us like him, but it does strengthen somewhat the impulse to pity him that we felt stirring at the end of Act 2.

Act III: Scene 3

Flint, another of the many castles that topped Welsh hills in those days of frequent petty warring, is the setting for this great scene. In under its ramparts march the Bolingbroke party—Bolingbroke himself, York, Northumberland, and a good show of military strength behind them. Bolingbroke and Northumberland are jubilant about the feebleness of the forces that rallied to Richard on his return from Ireland.

York is still holding aloof from them, psychologically if not physically. He reproves Northumberland for omitting Richard's title. When that arrogant Earl shows little concern about this breach of respect, York, in a fine flash of word play, reminds the Northerner of the time when such an offense would have brought Northumberland to the executioner's block.

> **COMMENT:** York has the old man's defect of dwelling too much on the past. He thinks too much about Richard's former glory and not enough of what can be done in the present to restore the glory and prestige of the monarchy. In fact, he hides from the present in his rosy dreams of the past. There is a family strain discernible in both York and Richard, uncle and nephew. They are both emotional, both escapists.

Bolingbroke and York exchange rather unfriendly warnings. Each cautions the other not to go too far. They are interrupted by young Harry Percy who had been sent ahead to demand the castle's submission. To their great surprise, they learn the King is there before them, and the castle, as Harry says, is "royally manned."

Bolingbroke, although taken quite off guard by this news, is able after only a minute's reflection to take the situation in hand. He orders that a message stating his allegiance be delivered to Richard. But attached to this promise of loyalty is a big "if." He will submit to Richard if Richard will repeal the exile sentence and restore the Lancaster lands and money. And there is a big "if not." If Richard will not come to terms, Bolingbroke will lay waste Richard's domain. He suggests that while the message is being delivered his men and equipment should be put through some military exercises on the plain below the castle. "Our fair appointments [strength] may be well perused [examined]" by the occupants of the castle. In the next breath after that hostile suggestion and even as he eyes with satisfaction his efficient troops, he says that he is quite willing to have Richard play the fiery, raging, dominant part. He himself would be content in a mild, unmenacing role.

Trumpets play the notes that indicate a parley or conference is to take place. The King appears on the ramparts.

> **COMMENT:** This is one of several places in the play where presumably Shakespeare is taking advantage of the upper level or balcony section of the Elizabethan stage. During the first part of this scene the actors playing Richard and his party stand on the balcony which could represent the top of the castle walls.

The Bishop of Carlisle, Aumerle, Scroop, and Salisbury stand around him. Bolingbroke points out the King to his friends. York gazes upward and comments, probably to himself, how kingly Richard *looks*. "Behold his eye / As bright as is the eagle's . . . . Alack, alack . . . / That any harm should stain so fair a show!"

> **COMMENT:** Bolingbroke's long speech and York's short one both continue themes now well established as important in the play. Bolingbroke brings us again the fire (sun)-water images. Bolingbroke refers to himself as a potential "crimson tempest," a rain of blood that will destroy England if Richard persists in refusing Bolingbroke's claims. Then he pictures himself as "yielding water," submissive to Richard's royal fire once Richard has satisfied his demands. Finally he compares Richard on the ramparts to a newly risen sun faced with opposing rain clouds that mean, says Bolingbroke (and no one could know more surely) "to stain . . . his bright passage."
>
> York compares Richard to an eagle. This grouping together of the images fire, sun, King, eagle is intentional. In the Elizabethan concept of the universe, each of these was chief in its class. Fire was the most important of the four elements; the sun was the chief planet; the King held primacy among men; the eagle was highest in the animal world.
>
> York also reminds us of the appearance-reality theme. Richard with his dramatic flair can, on occasion, *play* the part of a king, and play it very well. It is a "fair" show; but it *is* a show, a sort of pretense.

In accord with the appearance York noted, Richard does begin in fine kingly fashion. Bolingbroke and his aides have not made the ceremonious bow and genuflection demanded by the presence of royalty. And why not? Richard is stern and premptory. Is he not their king? If not, "who hath dismissed us from our stewardship?" He has, because of Bolingbroke's treachery, few earthly supporters. But "my master, God Omnipotent, / Is mustering in His clouds on our behalf / Armies of pestilence." The rebels will be punished and their sons and their sons' sons. Bolingbroke is trifling with "the purple testament of bleeding war." If he is not careful, he will cause the deaths of thousands of Englishmen.

Bolingbroke remains silent and at a distance from the castle. Northumberland moves to the base of the castle walls and replies for his chief. Looking up at Richard, Northumberland speaks according to his instructions. Bolingbroke swears by his close relationship to Richard and by the ancestral blood they have in common that all he wants is the cancellation of the exile sentence and the restoration of his property. Granted these two requests, he will become the peaceful, faithful servant of the King. Richard's reply is very strange. He instructs Northumberland to tell his "noble cousin" that "all the number of his fair demands / Shall be accomplished without contradiction." Is this the amazing capitulation to Bolingbroke that it sounds like? We soon learn positively that it is. Richard turns to Aumerle and says he feels that he debases himself by talking so mildly. He is tempted to call back Northumberland and send the other possible reply to Bolingbroke—a message of defiance and battle challenge. Aumerle counsels that it is best to stick to the friendly line and bide their time. Northumberland withdraws to confer with Bolingbroke.

Richard bewails his fate. That he should actually stoop to revoking the exile sentence! He wishes he could be as great as his title. Or failing that, that he could forget his past prestige, that he could ignore what he must now become. He does not give the returned Northumberland time to indicate Bolingbroke's decision. Instead he fires a barrage of questions, all showing that he expects Bolingbroke to dominate, perhaps depose him. He claims that he doesn't care. He is ready to relinquish all the symbols of his privileged position—his jewels, palace, robes, scepter, subjects. He is ready to exchange them all for humble substitutes—ready in fact to exchange his kingdom for a grave. He rambles off into a ridiculous image of himself and Aumerle weeping away until their tears have dug out their graves. Finally, he brings himself to attend to Northumberland's message that Bolingbroke awaits Richard in the lower court of the castle (probably an open air courtyard). Richard descends to "King Bolingbroke" (note that Richard himself is the first to crown, as it were, Bolingbroke), to the "base court, where kings grow base."

> **COMMENT:** The symbolic meaning of Richard's condescending to go to Bolingbroke and especially to go *down* to Bolingbroke is, of course, very obvious. It is reinforced by another sun image. Richard thinks of and applies to himself the sad myth of young Phaeton. Phaeton tried to be a sun god and failed disastrously.

As they wait for Richard to make his progress down inside the castle, Northumberland warns Bolingbroke that Richard, in his sorrow and grief, has been talking like a frantic (insane) man.

> **COMMENT:** This expression of awareness, at least, of Richard's weight of sorrow is surprising in the seemingly hardened Northumberland. At no other point in the play does he display any sensitivity at all. That he does here, even to this slight extent, is indirect testimony to the intensity of Richard's suffering.

RICHARD II

Now, his will having prevailed, Bolingbroke is punctilious in his respect to Richard. He drops to his knees as Richard advances into the courtyard. But Richard urges him to rise. "Your heart is up, I know, / Thus high [and here Richard levels his hand with his crown] at least, although your knee be low." Bolingbroke, in wounded tones, objects that he wants only what belongs to him. Richard passes over this obvious falsehood and on to the hard political fact that justifies Bolingbroke's usurpation. "They well deserve to have / That know the strongest and surest way to get." He then turns to comfort the weeping York. He tells Bolingbroke that he will do what he wants "for do we must what force will have us do."

SUMMARY. This is a high-powered scene and one of the most important in the play.

1) From the point of view of action, only one significant event occurs, but it is the climax event on which the whole plot pivots. This event is Richard's submission to Bolingbroke. The tension concerning the personal conflict between the two leaders now ebbs away. Bolingbroke has won; he is probably surprised himself how easily and quickly his victory came. But even though that tension has been dissipated, a new suspense builds up. What will become of Richard in this new arrangement?

2) The scene has tremendous psychological impact and depth. The royal submission is like an explosion in whose brief but awful glare each character is exposed for what he really is.

a. We see and hear *Northumberland's* insolence. We see also his competence which for the time being he puts at the service of Bolingbroke. But there is irony here. In years to come an older Bolingbroke, the King in *Henry IV, Part 1*, will suffer from the very traits that he now encourages in this strong man of the North.

b. We have renewed evidence of *York's* characteristic way of meeting the problem posed by Richard. He is reduced to lamentation and, at the end of the scene, open weeping. In this play Shakespeare shows us at least three ways of coping with an ineffectual leader. Gaunt's method was frank, fearless, but constructive criticism. Bolingbroke's method is as fearless as his father's, but quite different in nature (see d). York, as was clear early in the play, has not his brother's courage nor his directness (except for rare and brief occasions). Although he knows what is right, he cannot make sustained, direct opposition to the weakness of the King nor to the ambition of his other nephew Bolingbroke. To afford relief, then, to his pent-up anxiety, he uses a third method, that of emotional protest.

c. *Aumerle* has been giving Richard the support of his presence ever since Richard landed in Wales, but he does not seem wholeheartedly committed to the King. He is somewhat of an enigma, but it is easy to believe that he is still undecided about which cousin to really ally himself with. His one brief speech in this scene is ostensibly advice to Richard (to bide his time about provoking Bolingbroke and "to fight with gentle words"), but it would serve well to protect his line of retreat to Bolingbroke. He could claim that he had prevented Richard from making things hard for Bolingbroke.

d. *Bolingbroke* is shown as strongest in the very areas in which the King is weakest. He is resourceful and decisive. Learning that Richard is unexpectedly close at hand, he quickly thinks up a good line of action; then he follows it. He doesn't waste time weighing various alternatives (he has none of Richard's Hamlet-like qualities) or bewailing his fate. He is persistent in hammering at his two immediate objectives—the revocation of the exile sentence and the restoration of his property. He intends, of course, that the attainment of those objectives will be a stepping stone to greater power. He is a good judge of his cousin's character. He knows that if he is persistent and undeviating, Richard will give in. He is energetic. He is masterful. We feel that he looks with confidence to the future.

e. As a king, *Richard* is at his worst in this scene. He is ineffectual, painfully self-pitying, and self-dramatizing. Most conspicuous is his vacillation in his attiitudes toward Bolingbroke. In rapid succession, he plays at being several types of kings: he is the haughty, assured monarch; the deserted king, looking to God for vengeance; the conciliating king, extending fair terms to a petitioner; and finally, the despised, cast-off relic of a sovereign. These are all poses, of course; Richard desperately tries on one mask after another to avoid confronting the reality—his own true face, the face of an artist, a poet, an actor, not the face of one born to command as a king must command. Sensing as we do the masterfulness of Bolingbroke, it is difficult to blame Richard for the sudden and total collapse of his resistance to his rival. Not only does he grant Bolingbroke his two demands, but he virtually hands ovre his throne, crown, and sceptre to him. We should give him credit for being smart enough to see that Bolingbroke was bound to win out, but it is shocking to see Richard give up so easily. He seems self-destructive, increasingly so as the scene progresses.

Act III: Scene 4

At last we get relief from the succession of grim castles and fighting men in armor that are so conspicuous in the first three scenes of this act. We discover the Queen and her ladies in a garden at Langley (pronounced Lang' lee), York's estate a short distance north of London. The ladies try unsuccessfully to divert the Queen whose mind is naturally with her husband Richard and his fortunes. She has had no recent news of him. When a gardener with two assistants starts to work in one corner of the garden, the Queen moves over near him. Everyone, she says, is discussing the political situation. She will eavesdrop to hear what this trio has to say. The gardener gives his orders to his two helpers. One assistant should bind up the "unruly" branches of the apricot tree; they are bending down the tree with the weight of their Fruit. The other man is told to cut back "too fast growing" sprigs. The head gardener will himself pull up the weeds that "suck the soil's fertility." One of the assistants remarks that the three of them are doing a better job of keeping law and order in their domain than the King and his aides are doing on the national level. These rulers have let the "sea-walled garden" that is England become rank with weeds and undisciplined growth, "swarming with caterpillars." (The weeds, the wild growth, the caterpillars all refer to abuses that Richard has promoted or tolerated in his government and his officials.)

The gardener tells this assistant not to worry about the country's situation; some of the worst weeds have already been pulled up. Bolingbroke has disposed of the Earl of Wiltshire, Bushy, and Green. Furthermore, the King, who has been so neglectful of the garden (kingdom) entrusted to his care, so remiss in trimming and dressing his orchard of fruit trees (nobility), is now in the hands of Bolingbroke. It is likely that he will be deposed in favor of Bolingbroke.

The Queen can contain herself no longer. She bursts from her listening place and bitterly tongue-lashes the gardener. How does he "a little better thing than earth" dare suggest that the great Richard has fallen? Where did he hear such a report?

The gardener is apologetic. He does not like to bring bad news, but he insists that what he said is true. Richard is indeed in "the mighty hand of Bolingbroke." On the scale of fate, Richard's fortunes descend and Bolingbroke's rise. Let her hasten down to London. She will find that his words are true, common knowledge, in fact.

With a natural resentment that she seems to be the last to know of Richard's unhappy state, the Queen calls her ladies, telling them to prepare for the London trip. As she hurries away, she flings back at the gardener a spiteful remark: she hopes that the plants he is working on will all wither. He does not retort in kind, even inwardly. He wishes only that her unhappiness might be removed by so simple a thing as an effective curse. Then he transplants a seedling of rue. (Rue is a fragrant herb. In the symbolic language of flowers, it is associated with sorrow.) It marks the place where the Queen's tears fell—"in the remembrance of a weeping Queen."

> **COMMENT:** This allusion by the gardener to the language of flowers reminds us immediately of the Ophelia scene in *Hamlet*. As she distributes her flowers in her "mad scene," Ophelia gives rue to Queen Gertrude.

SUMMARY. Although seemingly rather insignificant, this scene makes important contributions to the general artistry of the plot. Among these contributions are the following:

1) It provides the illusion of a passage of time. Time is needed for Bolingbroke, Richard, and their followers to make the long ride from Flint Castle far in the west of England to the London area. Their specific goal is Westminster, the seat of the government, just outside London proper in those days. This journey would take several days.

2) It maintains the same sad and tense emotional atmosphere that prevails in the earlier scenes in the act, but it gives us the feminine emotional version in the reactions of the Queen. We observe the special nature of her sadness—her discontent and anxiety because she does not *know* what is going on. We also observe the rather shrill and abusive nature of her anger and her protesting disbelief when she *is* informed of the events. We hear the petty meanness of her curse against the inoffensive gardener. These various facets of her reaction seem psychologically true. They provide another dimension to the tragedy by showing that even the gentle nature of the Queen is being, in a sense, corrupted.

3) It presents in a half-dozen lines one of the remarkably perceptive and ennobling expressions of human experience that are a hallmark of Shakespeare's plays. The gardener, although maligned by the Queen, does not react bitterly. Instead, he understands and pities the grief that caused the Queen's unkindness. This is a kindly and noble attitude; but it is, as we happily recognize, a human one, too. Human beings are sometimes as sensitive and magnanimous as this gardener. We ourselves are influenced to adopt this tolerance for the afflicted Queen.

4) It also affords us the pleasure of one of the most imaginative passages in the play. This is the long, detailed comparison that sees England in terms of a garden. The patriotic theme is reintroduced subtly here. The three gardeners' love of England is manifested in their seeing her as a garden deserving careful attention. Symbolically they equate her with the most important trust of their own lives. They add another stanza to the paean of patriotic praise that we have heard from Gaunt, Richard, and others.

Act IV: Scene 1

Assembled in Westminster Hall is a group of high prelates, noblemen and magnates of the realm.

> **COMMENT:** It is rather ironic that Richard's formal deposition will take place in this particular building. It had just been completed. Richard had taken much interest in the designing and construction of it, as he did in most artistic activities. He had intended it to be one of the architectural triumphs of his reign.

The Bishop of Carlisle, the Abbot of Westminster, Bolingbroke, Aumerle, Northumberland, his son Harry Percy, and Bagot are all there. Other less important personages swell the attendance at this meeting which is presided over by Bolingbroke. Bolingbroke has already assumed some political and administrative powers. As the first business of the meeting, he is trying to discover the truth about the death of the Duke of Gloucester.

First, he urges Bagot to tell what he knows. Not at all loath and probably primed, Bagot accuses Aumerle. He actually claims to quote a boast that he says he heard Aumerle make about his ability to murder Gloucester.

He then caps that with the assertion that he heard Aumerle also wish for the death of Bolingbroke. Aumerle is hot in his denial and calls Bagot a liar. He throws down his glove as challenge to mortal combat, despite the fact that Bagot's blood is not noble. Ordinarily a nobleman would disdain to stain his knightly sword with base blood. Aumerle considers that the provocation excuses his breach of etiquette. But Bolingbroke will not let Bagot pick up the gage. Fitzwater, who *is* of noble blood, repeats the accusation of Aumerle and throws down his gage. Fitzwater and Aumerle exchange appropriately slanderous reflections on each other's integrity. Apparently Aumerle throws down his other glove to respond to Fitzwater's challenge. Harry Percy chimes in, on the other side of Fitzwater, of course; and another lord does also.

Then the Duke of Surrey, an older man who has been silent so far, berates Fitzwater for giving a false report to Aumerle's words prior to the assassination of Gloucester. Surrey heard them, too. According to him they were quite different from Fitzwater's version. A private but livel[y] quarrel develops between Surrey and Fitzwater. Mowbray's name dragged in as one who had held the opinion that Aumerle was really th[e] assassin. Aumerle, having used up both gloves, asks someone to lend hi[m] one. He wants to throw one down now as a challenge to the absent Mo[w]bray. Bolingbroke announces that Mowbray will be summoned home [to] give his testimony against Aumerle. Mowbray will also, says Bolingbrok[e] be reinstated in his property. (He had lost this at the time of his exile[.]) But Bolingbroke, who has been faring very well in this attack on Aume[rle] since Aumerle is a supporter of Richard, cannot have everything [his] way. The Bishop of Carlisle announces that Mowbray has concluded [his] honorable career as a valiant warrior. He has died in Italy, at Veni[ce] and has been buried there. So Bolingbroke tells the accusers and t[he] accused that they will be assigned days for their single combats.

York enters and informs Bolingbroke that "plume-plucked Richard" wish[es] to abdicate and to hand over the sceptre to Bolingbroke. Long like Ki[ng] Henry IV! Bolingbroke accepts. "In God's name I'll ascend the reg[al] throne."

The Bishop of Carlisle rises and addresses Bolingbroke and the other[s.] He admits that he is not the gifted speaker that some of them are, but hi[s] office demands that he assert the truth. There is no one there good enoug[h] in character or high enough in rank to judge "the noble Richard." The[y] are subjects of Richard and therefore not eligible to judge him. Also they are judging Richard in his absence, an injustice they would not inflict on common thieves. Their deed is "heinous, black, obscene." King Hereford (Bolingbroke) is a traitor to Hereford's King. Then the great prophecy rolls out that brings us back to the play's beginning, back to that farseeing, experienced old man, John of Gaunt. Although Carlisle speaks against Bolingbroke and Gaunt spoke against Richard, both really make the same point—that the welfare of England is being endangered, and that these present policies will cause trouble in the future. Carlisle foretells that if Bolingbroke proceeds with his usurpation of the throne, English blood will "manure" English ground, "future ages will groan for this foul act," "kin with kin" will war, and England will become another Golgotha.

COMMENT: This prophecy is all too true. It is a sort of capsule summary of the events covered in Shakespeare's chronicle plays *Henry IV, Parts 1, 2, Henry V, Henry VI, Parts 1, 2, 3,* and *Richard III.* Bolingbroke's seizure of Richard's throne and title was the root cause of the domestic (as opposed to foreign) troubles that distress England and her kings in each of these plays. It may be true that Shakespeare does not favor either Richard or Bolingbroke, but he certainly does emphasize the cold, hard reality of this historical fact.

Northumberland, apparently silently directed by Bolingbroke, promptly arrests the churchman for treason. This arrest, however, does not entail his imprisonment at this time. Bolingbroke orders that Richard be brought to the hall to make a public "surrender."

York reappears with Richard and officers who carry the royal crown and other symbols of sovereignty. Richard is in a distressed and a distressing state when he enters. His self-control improves as the scene progresses. At this point, he complains that he hasn't yet learned to act like a subject, especially to those men who, Judas-like, did him reverence so short a time before.

COMMENT: More than once Richard makes allusions in which, by implication, he compares himself to the betrayed Christ.

Anyway, why has he been sent for? York, firmly, as if speaking to a peevish child, reminds Richard that he has come to resign his state and crown to Henry Bolingbroke. Richard has himself indicated that he wants to do this.

Richard picks up the crown. He looks at Bolingbroke and tells him that the crown is like a deep well which has two buckets, his and Bolingbroke's. His is the one that is submerged, "full of tears." ("This is another water image. Richard, now associated with water, is no longer symbolized by fire or sun.)

COMMENT: Bolingbroke is used to his cousin's flowery flights of fancy, and he is prepared for vacillation in Richard. He sees that he must try to hold Richard to the point at issue. In the conversation that follows, Richard delivers several long and exasperatingly evasive speeches. After each one Bolingbroke or his ally Northumberland try to recall Richard to the matter at hand. Finally they do succeed, but not, we suspect, until Richard wants them to. Richard's motive is not fully clear. He may be still as distraught as he seemed when he entered and unable to focus his attention; he may be eager to make the points expressed in these speeches and determined to do so, whatever Bolingbroke's plans may be; he may

purposely be annoying Bolingbroke. At any rate, by the end of the
scene we feel that the psychological victory has gone to Richard.
He says what he wants to say, despite Bolingbroke. Bolingbroke has,
of course, the political victory; but Richard strengthens as the scene
progresses and acquires a dignity he never had in his prosperity.

Richard says that he does intend to yield his crown, but he is keeping
his griefs. Bolingbroke points out that Richard is handing over heavy
cares with his crown. Richard plays with the word "care"; then he plays
with Bolingbroke's feelings when the latter tries to pin him down. "Are
you contented to resign the crown?" "Aye, no—no, aye," retorts Richard,
unhelpfully. In a litany type of list Richard enumerates what he is relinquishing—the crown's "heavy weight," "the unwieldy sceptre," the
balm that consecrated him at the time of his coronation, pomp, majesty,
manors, rents, decrees, statutes. They all go to Bolingbroke "that hast all
achieved." And now, he inquires, what else do they want him to do?
Northumberland presents him with a prepared statement of guilt which
they want him to read. Richard says Northumberland has his own guilt.
It includes the deposing of a king. He and the other onlookers are so
many hand-washing Pilates. But theirs is a guilt no water can wash away.

COMMENT: Earlier in this play (Act III, Scene 1) we have an
image of bloodstained hands. Before he orders their deaths, Bolingbroke says to Bushy and Green "to wash your blood / From off my
hands . . . / I will unfold some causes of your deaths." Here we
have a very similar image of hands deeply stained with guilt, in this
case stained beyond water's power to cleanse. Shakespeare was to
re-use this type of image in the even more famous passage in
Macbeth. Macbeth, fresh from the murder of Duncan, looks with
horror at his bloodstained hands. "Will all great Neptune's ocean
wash the blood / Clean from my hand? No, this my hand will
rather / The multitudinous seas incarnadine, / Making the green one
red."

Richard delays and delays, by no means daunted by Northumberland,
"thou haught, insulting man." He suggests again, as he does early in the
scene, his wish for death. This time it is in another fire-water image. He
wishes he were a king of snow who could melt away to water drops before the sun of Bolingbroke. Then he startles them all by asking for a
mirror to study his face; has it changed since he gave up his sovereignty?
Bolingbroke orders the mirror to be brought, and Northumberland again
offers the paper for Richard to read, while the glass is being fetched. Richard turns on Northumberland in real anger and calls him a tormenting
fiend. Bolingbroke, who probably agrees, tells Northumberland "to urge
it no more." Richard examines his face in the mirror and marvels that it
is the same face that he had in his days of power. "Was this the face /
That, like the sun, did make beholders wink?"

COMMENT: There is an echo here of a famous line in *The Tragical History of Dr. Faustus*, a play written by Shakespeare's gifted predecessor Christopher Marlowe. Marlowe wrote of Helen of Troy, "Was this the face that launched a thousand ships / And burnt the topless towers of Ilium?"

His scrutiny ended, Richard smashes the glass as a sort of symbol of the destruction he at least half-wishes for himself. The prosaic Bolingbroke, moved perhaps more than he had expected to be by the pathos of the occasion, makes a poetic and perceptive observation: "The shadow of your sorrow hath destroyed / The shadow of your face." This states very well Richard's fatal addiction to pretense, to living with shadows instead of substance and fact. Its particular reference is to his breaking of the mirror (the shadow of his face) in a flashy theatrical gesture (the shadow of his sorrow). Richard is generous enough to admit both the beauty and the truth of his rival's remark. His "external manners" are "merely shadows to the unseen grief / That swells in silence in the tortured soul." He asks the new King one boon, and Bolingbroke promises to grant it. Richard wants to depart—any place so long as he is out of their sight. Bolingbroke gives an order that he be taken to the Tower of London.

COMMENT: The Tower is one of London's oldest structures. Built originally as a fortress, it also served for centuries as a prison, especially for those accused of political crimes.

Bolingbroke sets the following Wednesday as his coronation day and sweeps out, followed by most of the others. But the Bishop of Carlisle, the Abbot of Westminster, and Aumerle linger. They are ripe for revolt against Bolingbroke, and the Abbot divulges that he already has plans afoot. But they must assure him of their good faith by receiving the sacrament of the Eucharist. Then he will disclose his plot "that will show us a merry day."

SUMMARY. This long scene is, of course, extremely important. It is the only scene in its act and therefore must by itself present all the adjustments usually found in the fourth act of a five-act tragedy. These adjustments are demanded by the climax events of the third act.

1) The main adjustment is Richard's.

a. He must first adjust to his admission of Bolingbroke's superiority. Shall he formally abdicate? His submission to his cousin at Flint Castle indicated that he would, but he must decide definitely. This scene gives the decision which constitutes his adjustment. He does abdicate (he says he is willing to resign his crown), but he cloaks and obscures his act with so much descriptive and digressive talk that we are scarcely aware of the act of abdication. This is Richard's characteristic way of handling unpleasant situations.

b. He must also adjust to being a subject instead of a ruler. His entrance speech stresses this difficulty. It lies not just in getting used to living without all the special services and privileges of a monarch, but also in accepting the harsh fact that his former retainers were time-serving hypocrites who now have turned against him.

c. At the scene's end he makes a most important adjustment. It is a psychological adjustment to himself. Having given up trying to be a king, he is able to look directly at himself, able to find the "substance" of himself. What he finds is a soul swollen with "unseen grief." The calm dignity with which he says these words conveys the satisfaction of real self-knowledge, a satisfaction that even his grief does not disturb.

2) Bolingbroke must also adjust to Richard's third act capitulation, but the adjustment involves no wrench. It amounts only to putting into effect a program already in his mind.

a. At the beginning of the scene he feels very confident that he will be able to move Richard on from the submission at Flint to formal abdication. So his adjustment is primarily to get down to the work of ruling even before he has the formal powers. He, therefore, attacks the unfinished business of finding Gloucester's murderer.

b. He does have to adjust to his new relationship to the nobles. He is now not only their leader but their prospective king. With most of them he is able to establish a favorable relationship. They accept his decisions about their quarrels early in the scene; they raise no objection to his treatment of Richard later in the scene. He is quick to subdue opposition to his authority, as is shown by the arrest of the Bishop of Carlisle. He intends to keep his nobles in line, and he feels that he can do so.

c. He finds his future prospects excellent as he prepares for his coronation.

3) Of the others involved in this scene, most seem to make the courtier's easy adjustment to a new regime. Four require closer attention.

a. *Bagot* has deserted Richard and is seeking the favor of Bolingbroke. He hopes to win it by disgracing Aumerle whom Bolingbroke considers a Richard supporter. He seems to be inventing false charges in the effort to curry favor with the new king.

b. *Aumerle* has no time to work out a personal adjustment to Richard's submission. Before he can make any attempt to improve his position, he finds himself suddenly the object of attack from the Bolingbroke faction, accused of his uncle Thomas of Gloucester's death. Aumerle is probably completely innocent of this crime. He is forced to stay on Richard's side, but he is not enthusiastic about it. It is notable that he has nothing to say in support of Richard during the abdication part of the scene. He does, however, fall in with the conspiracy against Bolingbroke; but he does not do so with any strong convictions, as later events are to prove.

c. *The Bishop of Carlisle* is unique in his adjustment. His position is actually a refusal to adjust. His views agree with those of York, but his courage in defense of them is far sturdier. He attacks the whole idea of submission and abdication. He puts his finger on the weak point—Bolingbroke is, in fact, a usurper. He spells out the disaster that such highhanded seizure of power can cause.

d. The Abbot of Westminster, whispering at the scene's end to his fellow conspirators, shows a sinister adjustment to the new regime, an adjustment that threatens Bolingbroke. It creates tension when weighed against Bolingbroke's confident reference to his coming coronation.

Curious about the outcome of the incipient revolt and concerned about the fate of the displaced Richard, we move into the final act in considerable suspense, even though the main conflict of the plot has been decided in favor of Bolingbroke, King Henry IV.

Act V: Scene 1

The Queen and her ladies have arrived in London. They have stationed themselves in one of the narrow streets that lead to the Tower of London. They await Richard who, they have learned, will be taken this way to his imprisonment. Soon the Queen sees Richard approaching. She finds him much altered, a withered "rose."

> **COMMENT:** The Queen's speeches in this scene are full of imagery, as rich in similes and metaphors as Richard's often are. This luxuriance of symbolism is partly planned by Shakespeare as appropriate for these two characters. Richard and his lady represent to some extent the aesthetic values of life as opposed to the prosaic realism of Bolingbroke. But the wealth of symbolism is also due to the place of this play in the evolution of Shakespeare's genius. At this stage he is in the process of learning how to combine his poetic and dramatic gifts. Eventually he will discipline himself to a blending of drama and poetry never surpassed in western literature. In this play, however, he is not quite the master of his poetic power. The poetic inventiveness is sometimes too obtrusive.

Richard speaks tenderly to the Queen. He asks her to refrain from grief. He says she must learn to look back on their former life as a happy dream. They are to be parted; he must walk alone now, with "grim necessity," towards death. He counsels her to seek refuge in a convent in France. The Queen protests that he cannot be so completely transformed. Has Bolingbroke deprived him of his intellect as well as everything else? Will he really take all this injustice mildly and without resistance?

Richard does not respond to her effort to shame him into action. He repeats his advice that she go back to her native France, leaving him, in effect, on his deathbed. In years to come, as people tell sad tales of an evening by winter firesides, she will be able to cap all their stories with her "lamentable tale" of "the deposing of a rightful king."

Northumberland brusquely interrupts. The orders for Richard's imprisonment have been changed (probably because rumors of the conspiracy have reached the ears of Bolingbroke). He is to go to Pomfret (Pontefract) Castle in northern England. The Queen is ordered to depart immediately for France. As on earlier occasions, Richard shows a strong aversion to Northumberland. This Percy, says Richard, is the ladder by which Bolingbroke has climbed to the throne. But this collaboration will not persist. They will quarrel; each will become jealous and fearful of the other; each will have learned from this Richard episode the extent of the villainy of which the other is capable.

> **COMMENT:** All this prophecy is actually realized in the Percy rebellion in *Henry IV, Part 1*. This passage, therefore, is an artistic and useful foreshadowing; but it is not really in character for Richard to be so discerning and correct in his analysis of people.

Northumberland is not alarmed and orders the husband and wife to part. Richard says he is twice divorced—of his crown and his wife. He must leave her to go to the chill North. She will return to her homeland, France, from which she came a girl, sweet as Maytime. She returns to it touched by the frosts of autumn.

Lovingly, the couple kiss and try to make their farewells. Her request to share Richard's banishment is refused by Northumberland. Richard gives additional evidence of his new grasp of reality, for it is he who moves to terminate the painful conversation. He is even able to see that their repeated endearments make their love and grief seem frivolous.

SUMMARY. This rather short scene supplies important information and provides considerable emotional enrichment.

1) The Queen has arrived in London in time to see and talk to Richard.

2) Richard is to be actually imprisoned. He is not merely to be detained in some kind of comfortable custody.

3) There is a strong indication that Bolingbroke's confidence may already be somewhat shaken. He is resorting to measures that smack of fear.

a. The deposed King and the Queen are treated ruthlessly. They are forced to make their final farewell to each other on the public roadway. They are limited to a few minutes with the impatient Northumberland as their grudging timekeeper.

b. Richard is to be removed far away, to remote Yorkshire, well away from any London sympathizers.

c. The Queen who might enlist the aid of such sympathizers is to be hustled out of the country, home to France.

These actions of Bolingbroke are especially significant because we have just listened to Richard's prophetic words to Northumberland, words that foretell trouble for Bolingbroke.

4) Emotionally this scene is favorable to Richard.

a. We see that his Queen loves him deeply and that he reciprocates her affection. They have had a happy married life, he says, so happy that it seems now like a dream-world.

b. Because he is cherished by the Queen, we find him more admirable.

c. Richard conducts himself well here. He is sympathetic; he is considerate of the Queen's grief and concerned about her future welfare. He is burdened with his own troubles, but he is no longer so self-centered that he is insensitive to the troubles of others. He does not let himself indulge in a maudlin, self-dramatizing performance.

Act V: Scene 2

The Duke of York and his Duchess discuss at their Langley estate the recent political events. The Duke has been telling his wife of the entry of Bolingbroke and Richard into London, at the end of the trip from Flint Castle. His tearful reaction to the situation still persists, and his recital has been interrupted by a fit of weeping. The Duchess, however, is naturally eager to hear the news. She implores him to get control of his feelings and to continue. She reminds him that he broke off at the description of the crowd's insolence toward Richard. They threw dirt and rubbish on his head as he rode along. York does resume. Bolingbroke had the crowd's hearty applause as he spurred his fiery but well-controlled horse through the streets. So alive were the buildings with onlookers and so noisy and hearty their welcome to Bolingbroke that it seemed the very windows and walls were saluting him. Bolingbroke acknowledged the greetings with low bows from his saddle.

But what about poor Richard, the lady inquires. Her husband rejoins that he suffered the fate of the second-rate actor who follows a star act.

> **COMMENT:** Shakespeare's references to his own profession are always very interesting. This one reminds us of the much longer passage in *Hamlet* (Act 3, Scene 2) where we learn some of Shakespeare's standards for good acting.

He received contempt and mistreatment. But he bore the hostility with patience and with smiles despite his tears. So pitiful was he that the only explanation of the crowd's enmity toward him must be that Heaven so designed it. At any rate, York is accepting that convenient explanation; he reminds his wife that he has sworn allegiance to Bolingbroke.

Aumerle approaches, and York informs his wife that Aumerle must be now called Rutland. Bolingbroke has reduced him from Duke of Aumerle to Earl of Rutland because of Aumerle's association with Richard. York has become pledge for his son's loyalty to Bolingbroke. The father and mother try to get Aumerle to talk court gossip, but he is not interested. York spies a seal, the type used on important documents, sticking out of the young man's shirt and asks what it is. Aumerle hastily conceals it with "My lord, 'tis nothing." Suspicious, York insists on seeing the paper. The more the father insists, the stronger the son's refusal to show the paper. Finally, York is able to snatch it, takes a rapid glance down the page and cries, "Treason! Foul treason! Villain! Traitor! Slave!" A servant is sent posthaste to get York's riding boots and to saddle his horse. The Duchess receives no answer to her startled queries as to what's wrong except "Peace, foolish woman!" "I will not peace!" she rejoins and appeals to her son for an explanation. She gets nothing from him except a frightening "It is no more than my poor life must answer." York is still yelling for his boots. He must ride immediately to the King. The Duchess tries to remonstrate with her husband.

> **COMMENT:** The Duchess is a strong-minded woman. Furthermore, her maternal instincts are aroused. Although she has none of the facts, she realizes that York intends to expose their son to the King's vengeance. Her son's life is to be endangered because of these political games the men are playing. Not if she can prevent it! She shows the same feminine valuation of family over political ties that the Duchess of Gloucester showed early in the play. They follow the same basic logic in their arguments: they oversimplify the political problems, but they also go to the human heart of the matter and champion fundamental human values.

Surely, he isn't going to publicize his own son's errors? And his only son, too. They have no others and, of course, cannot expect more children at their age. Will he injure her by taking away her "fair son"—the son who so resembles himself?

York calls her "mad" and "fond" (which meant "foolish"). Would she conceal this conspiracy, sworn on the sacrament of the altar, this conspiracy to kill the King (Bolingbroke now) when he arrives at Oxford? The Duchess does not take a stand about the conspiracy; it doesn't much interest her. But Aumerle does, and, she says, they can just keep him at home at Langley so he can't go to Oxford. This plan is just further evidence to York of her "fondness." He declares that if Aumerle were twenty times his son, he'd accuse him. The Duchess tries another approach. She knows why York is so pitiless; he suspects that Aumerle is not his son, but a bastard. "Sweet York, sweet husband, be not of that mind!" He is the image of York, obviously his son; he doesn't resemble her or her family. But this trick of pretended hurt fails. York pushes her aside and leaves.

The mother turns to Aumerle. She urges him also to ride off to London, if possible, to outride his father and get to King Henry first with a confession of whatever crime he has committed. And she herself will follow. She's old, it is true, but she can still keep pace with York. She will throw herself at the feet of Bolingbroke and not rise until Aumerle is pardoned.

SUMMARY. This and the one that follows are very good scenes.

1) A common opinion is that Shakespeare intended them to be humorous, although the family distress is genuine and the situation certainly is dangerous for Aumerle. Some critics have questioned the artistry of introduc-

ing what amounts to a small comic sub-plot at this late point in the play. These two scenes are, in fact, sometimes omitted in the stage productions. Perhaps they do disturb the smooth tragic flow of events and moods in the two final acts. But Shakespeare's microcosm (the little world of his plot) always suggests the complexity of the macrocosm (the great world of human society and its environment). And society *is* a complex of tragic and comic, of domestic and public concerns, of the trivial and the important. In his major tragedies Shakespeare is careful to suggest this same complexity. When he wrote them, he had developed added skill and so may integrate his humorous material more effectively. The following examples come to mind easily:

a. In the graveyard scene in *Hamlet* (Act 5, Scene 1), we laugh at the gravediggers' rough jokes and even at some of Hamlet's observations; but, as they jest, the men dig the grave of Ophelia whose death is one of the most pathetic aspects of the play's tragedy.

b. In the drunken porter scene in *Macbeth* (Act 2, Scene 3), we are amused by the tipsy, grumpy fumbling of the porter in responding to the urgent knocking of MacDuff and Lennox; but that loud knocking is a sort of alarm to alert the world that murder has been done—King Duncan lies stabbed.

c. In the disrobing scene in *Othello* (Act 4, Scene 1), we are diverted by Emilia's earthy realism and by the contrast between her point of view about marriage and Desdemona's shining idealism; but that idealism and innocence help to cause the almost unbearably poignant death that Desdemona soon suffers.

In each of these, as in the *Richard II* material, the comedy is closely mingled with the tragic elements, suggesting the serio-comic nature of many life experiences. They are not unintegrated, dangling farce episodes, thrown in exclusively to pander to the low tastes of some in the audience. It is true, of course, that they all do provide some welcome relief after much tense tragedy; but they have also the artistic and moral significance explained above.

2) They present an intrepid female character, the Duchess of York. She is more fully realized and more real to us than either the Queen or the Duchess of Gloucester. She is a character we relate to easily. We like her pluck and her persistence, even though we may think her a little ridiculous. We find her common-sense, if rather limited, view a refreshing change from the high-level politics we have been contending with. It is especially gratifying to find one character valiant enough to oppose Bolingbroke as this lady does in the next scene. There is ironic relish to the fact that it is not only a woman but a woman of purely domestic interests who performs this feat.

3) This first of the two companion scenes is a diverting study of family life. It starts with a quiet, companionable talk between husband and wife. He relates to her the latest news. He makes the candid revelation of his real feelings that is usually possible only within the family circle. Then,

in abrupt contrast to this peaceful, low-pitched beginning, we have trouble —a family squabble. It follows a familiar pattern—father versus son with mother trying to make peace but favoring the son. Of course, the issues, treachery and possible execution are more portentous than the causes of most family quarrels.

4) These scenes bring up again the interpretation of Aumerle's character. In this scene he pursues his usual policy of saying as little as possible. This policy certainly suggests that he wants to avoid committing himself.

Act V: Scene 3

King Henry (Bolingbroke) complains to his lords at Windsor Castle about his spendthrift son, Prince Hal. He says he hasn't laid eyes on him for three months. He hears reports that the young man hangs out in the London taverns; and "they" say that he and the low dissolute companions he has taken up with amuse themselves by beating the patrolling watchmen and robbing pedestrians. The youthful Harry Percy tells the King of a chance conversation he had a couple of days before with the Prince. They had talked about the tournament scheduled for Oxford.

> **COMMENT:** This type of tournament could be described as a chivalric sports event. The contestants had to be knights. They fought a series of mock combats with blunted weapons, and prizes were awarded at the end to those showing the most skill. It was customary for each knight to wear a token given him by his lady love, such as a glove, a sash, or a ribbon.

The Prince flippantly announced his intention of entering the competition wearing a common prostitute's glove as his token. The King shakes his head and says that the Prince is as bold as he is dissolute; but there have been evidences of real worth in the young man's character, and on these the father pins his hopes for the future.

> **COMMENT:** These comments about Prince Henry constitute skillful foreshadowing; for this is the engaging Prince Hal who plays so prominent a part in *Henry IV, Part 1* and *Part 2*, the Prince Hal who becomes on the death of his father the admirable King Henry V, the hero of the play by that name. This reference prepares readers or viewers for the two rather different facets of Hal's personality—(1) the wild recklessness of his early days of boon companionship with men like the wonderful rogue Falstaff; (2) the underlying seriousness, stability, and loyalty shown in his combat with Hotspur, his sober acceptance of the duties of monarch, and his great leadership at the battle of Agincourt.

All of a sudden, Aumerle rushes in with a distraught look immediately noted by his cousin the King. He begs the King for a private conference. The others withdraw, and Aumerle throws himself on his knees insisting that he will never rise until he has Bolingbroke's pardon. Bolingbroke says he'll get the pardon if the crime, whatever it is, has not actually been committed. He agrees to Aumerle's suggestion that they lock the door while Aumerle explains. But there comes a frantic pounding at the door, and York's voice warns the King: "Thou hast a traitor in thy presence. . . . / Open the door, or I will break it open." Bolingbroke draws his sword and admits York who hands him the incriminating document. Aumerle reminds the King of the pardon (or so he interprets it) just extended. Bolingbroke and York take turns in berating Aumerle. The father's indignation is just as hot as the King's. "Forget to pity him, lest thy pity prove / A serpent that will sting thee to the heart!" cries York, and "Mine honor lives when his dishonor dies." "Oh loyal father of a treacherous son," compliments Bolingbroke.

> **COMMENT:** York's known devotion to the Divine Right of Kings may partially excuse him here for his unnatural attack on his son. But in his shrill vituperation most readers hear also a good deal of self-interest and desire to make it very clear that he is in no way connected with his son's crime. This craven streak is consistent with earlier actions of York, but he is more shameful here than ever before. His desertion of Richard has caused a real deterioration in his character.

Now, there is more hammering on the door and more shouting. It is the redoubtable Duchess. She implores the King to admit her, a "beggar." The melodramatic aspects of the situation begin to amuse the King, who tells Aumerle, "my dangerous cousin," to let his mother in. As she enters, York is still urging the "cutting off" of Aumerle. Immediately, the Duchess begs the King to ignore York, really a dangerous man to everyone since he can be so unnatural to his own son. The family tempest surges around the King. Soon all three, father, mother, and son, are on their knees before him. Aumerle, as usual, is almost silent. But his parents, especially his mother, are abundantly vocal. The chief line of argument of the Duchess is that York must be only pretending, and she is in dead, dead earnest. But probably her most effective weapon against Bolingbroke is her refusal to stand up. Bolingbroke doesn't try to say much, but three times he does beseech her, "Rise up, good Aunt." "Do not say 'Stand up.' / Say 'Pardon' first," she interjects between two stages of her verbal barrage.

So Bolingbroke says it: "I pardon him, as God shall pardon me." The Duchess rejoices in the superiority, as she puts it, that her inferior kneeling position has given her. But she demands that Bolingbroke repeat his pardon to make it "strong." And the King does: "With all my heart / I pardon him." But there will be no pardon for the other conspirators. York is empowered to raise a force to seize them at Oxford or wherever else they are hiding out. The King then bids the whole family farewell with a compliment to the Duchess for her maternal love and a charge to Aumerle to try to be loyal.

SUMMARY. This scene is full of family tensions and conflicts between generations, but despite this, it is comparatively lighthearted in tone and atmosphere.

1) King Henry worries about his wayward son who deserts the court and sows his wild oats among disreputable companions, but the manner in which he expresses his worry shows his love for his son. This love is further emphasized by the father's confidence that there really is promise in Hal.

2) It is clear that much of the trouble between the King and the Prince is to be ascribed to the young fellow's desire to lead his own life away from the restrictions and supervision of the family setting, in this case the court. The King, although anxious, seems to understand that this is an episode of temporary rebellion.

3) Harry Percy is, in this play, a model youth. His part is small and his speeches few, but in all of them he is respectful to his elders, well-mannered and decorous. He becomes a sort of foil here for Hal. In the next chronicle plays of *Henry IV Part 1* and *Part 2*, this young Percy becomes a more rebellious and more interesting character. He continues the role of opposite number to Hal, but only in the sense that they are political enemies. Each is a spirited young man, and each learns to respect the other. Hal grieves when he kills Harry Percy (Hotspur) in fair combat on the battlefield of Shrewsbury, and we grieve, too.

4) The York family fights out its tensions all too publicly along the lines summarized at the end of the previous scene. Again a strained father-son relationship is portrayed. York, of course, has considerably more to complain of in Aumerle than Bolingbroke has in Prince Hal; but, even making allowances for that, York's handling of his erring son is hysterical and unpleasant.

5) This is one of Bolingbroke's best scenes. He is, for a while, at least, a really sympathetic character.

a. He worries about his son but does not reject him.

b. After an initial fright, he is sensibly calm and detached during the York family fracas.

c. He is kindly to the Duchess and seems really to admire her love and courage, although definitely distressed by her conduct.

d. He is generous to Aumerle. He probably knows his cousin well enough to realize that neither Richard nor anyone else will ever have a very ardent supporter in Aumerle.

Shakespeare does not want to cast Bolingbroke in the role of complete villain. He is a monarch of England. Shakespeare lived under another English monarchy, one that was sensitive about royal rights and dignities. Furthermore, Shakespeare's Queen Elizabeth had, because of her descent from Henry VII who was partly a Lancaster, some sympathy with the

Lancaster cause, that is Bolingbroke's cause. Shakespeare, like other Elizabethan writers, would certainly avoid offending his queen.

Act V: Scene 4

Sir Pierce (Peter) of Exton, a nobleman who has not previously figured in the play, is consulting with his servant. They are in Windsor Castle and are discussing recent remarks of King Henry. As quoted by Exton, Bolingbroke had said twice, and with some urgency, "Have I no friend will rid me of this living fear?" The servant agrees that these were the King's exact words. After these words were said by Bolingbroke, Exton had then felt that the King's eyes, ranging over the listening group of courtiers, had settled meaningfully on him, as if he were saying, "I would thou wert the man / That would divorce this terror from my heart." Exton supplies the explanation of what the King meant by "terror." He says that Bolingbroke is referring to that other "King," the man who lies imprisoned at Pomfret. And I am, indeed, "the King's friend, and will rid his foe," declares Exton. "Come, let's go."

SUMMARY. This very short (eleven lines) scene makes a contribution to the play out of proportion to its brevity.

1) It forwards the plot action tremendously. An attempt is going to be made on the life of Richard.

2) It follows the line of the previous scene in treating Bolingbroke's character, considering the circumstances, rather favorably. It relieves the King of the full guilt of Richard's death. Exton has received no direct command from Bolingbroke. He is acting on his own initiative, on the basis of what he thinks Bolingbroke meant. From what Bolingbroke later admits, Exton was right in his interpretation of what the King *wished*, but he acted before Bolingbroke really decided to implement that wish. The fact that Exton is seeking some corroboration for his impressions of what Bolingbroke really said and meant casts added doubt on his understanding of the situation. Exton's conviction that Bolingbroke singled him out by a look is so purely subjective that we can give it little weight as evidence of Bolingbroke's guilty intentions.

3) It introduces a new character, minor in the extent of his role but vastly important in the play's denouement (final unraveling of the plot). Already in this short scene we get an idea of Exton's character. He is unscrupulous, certainly. He professes himself King Henry's friend. If he is, he is the stupid, shortsighted kind of friend who is worse than an avowed enemy. More likely he is his own friend who wants to impress Bolingbroke and so make his mark at court. The fact that he turns to a servant to discuss such an important matter would make the Elizabethan audience, and probably their modern counterpart also, distrust him.

4) By the subtle touch in the last two lines of using "King" to apply first to Richard and then to Bolingbroke, Shakespeare reminds us again of the

fundamental political problem of the play. Which really *was* the King now: the incompetent but anointed Richard or the competent but usurping Bolingbroke?

Act V: Scene 5

Richard, in solitary confinement in dismal Pomfret Castle, begins this dolorous scene with a long soliloquy. He says he has been considering how he can compare his prison cell to the world. Of course, the world is thronged with people, and his cell is empty save for himself. But he won't be thwarted. By the combined labor of his mind and soul, he will produce thoughts and ideas to people his lonely room. Thoughts are like people—complex, everchanging, full of humors.

> **COMMENT:** "Humor" (or "humour") was an important word in Renaissance science, both physiological and psychological. It referred to the four basic fluids of which it was believed the human body was compounded. The individual's temperament at any given time was, according to this theory, the result of the predominance of one of these fluids in his physical make-up. For instance, if one had a predominance of black bile, one would be melancholic in temperament. Although science has proved this theory untenable, it does have the merit of recognizing the interaction of body and psyche, of recognizing the psychosomatic nature of illness. As Richard uses "humors" here, he means that various kinds of thoughts, some comforting and some painful, come to his mind.

The highest kind of thoughts, those concerned with religion, usually are accompanied by disturbing scruples. He thinks of the Bible's reassuring "Come, little ones."* But then comes the memory of the stern warning that it is easier for a camel to go through the eye of a needle than for a rich man to enter heaven.**

Richard continues tracing his thoughts. Sometimes he thinks of escape, of tearing out his prison walls with his fingernails. This brave thought dies of frustration. Next come thoughts intended to soothe: he is not the first to suffer in this way, nor will he be the last. In his present mood, Richard regards this kind of thinking as weak, fitting for a beggar in the stocks, perhaps; but a king should not transfer his burdens to the backs of others who may have endured the same punishment.

---

*He probably has in mind the words of Jesus in Matthew, Chapter 19: "Suffer little children, and forbid them not to come to me."

**Shakespeare's eye is still on Matthew, Chapter 19: "And again I say unto you, it is easier for a camel to go through the eye of a needle, than for a rich man to enter into the kingdom of heaven." The fact that the two passages come from the same chapter accentuates the contrast that Richard feels in them.

COMMENT: Note here particularly how well Richard can now discern the difference between appearance and reality and how decided is his choice of reality, even bitter reality.

In entertaining these thoughts, he is, as he says, playing "many people." But actually his development of this idea shows that what he ponders is two people: Richard, the monarch; and Richard, the subject. Which is better off? When he thinks of himself as King, the fear of treason makes him prefer to be a beggar. But the fear of poverty swings back his preference to the throne. Then he recollects that in point of fact he is "unkinged," and unkinged by Bolingbroke. This makes him feel very depressed —"and straight am nothing." But the climax of his meditation is the realization that no human being will ever be content "till he be eased / With being nothing," until death has released him.

Richard hears music, or rather dissonance produced by an untalented player. He hates this ugly distortion of good music. Equally hateful, he says, is the distortion of a human life. He, although he has a fine delicate ear for music, did not hear soon enough the grating distortions in the music of his own life. He failed to "keep time" in his living. And then, switching to another meaning of time (note, again, the Elizabethan introduction of puns into very serious material), he laments, "I wasted time, and now Time doth waste me." He indulges next in a complicated, too-clever image, comparing his thoughts to minutes, his eyes to watches, his finger to the watch hands on the dial, his groans to chimes, and his heart to the bell itself. It all adds up to the point that time drags for him and that it is punctuated by his sighs, groans, and tears.

Again the music sounds, and he shouts out "let it sound no more." He has heard that music is sometimes used therapeutically to cure the insane, but the kind that he is hearing now will have just the opposite effect. Yet, he reminds himself that he should really appreciate this sound, for the playing is well-intentioned. Someone is trying to alleviate his loneliness. It is a gesture of love, and he gets little love these days "in this all-hating world."

COMMENT: Notice the dramatic effectiveness of this phrase as a herald of the atrocity that is to follow.

Someone enters the dark cell and salutes Richard. "Hail, royal Prince." Richard retorts ironically, "Thanks, noble peer." The man's dress shows that he belongs to the servant class, but Richard wants to express his new philosophy that all men are about equal. Richard inquires who the man is. A visitor is most unusual. Ordinarily Richard sees only "that sad dog (his jailer) / That brings me food to make misfortune live." The newcomer explains that he had been a groom in Richard's royal stable. He is on a trip north to York and had gone to great difficulty to get the necessary permission to visit Richard. He wants to look again on Richard's face.

As he talks to Richard, the groom relates how unhappy he had been on the recent coronation day to see the new king riding the very "roan Barbary" horse* that Richard used to ride. Often had this groom curried and prepared him for Richard. Richard inquires with interest how the horse acted with his new rider. The groom has to admit that the Barbary pranced as "proudly as if he disdained the ground." Richard is hurt. The horse might have shown more gratitude for Richard's kindness to him, the treats of tasty food, the rewarding pats. Couldn't he at least stumble and break Boilngbroke's neck? But good sense reasserts itself. Why blame the horse whose nature it is to bear burdens? Why not blame himself? Contrary to what is right for his royal nature, he has allowed Bolingbroke to load him like an ass, to spur and weary him.

As the keeper enters, the groom leaves. The jailer wants Richard to eat some food he has brought. Richard tells him to taste it first, their usual procedure to assure Richard that he is not being poisoned; but the keeper refuses. He has been commanded not to by Sir Pierce of Exton, just arrived "from the King." Richard flares up. "The Devil take Henry of Lancaster and thee! / Patience is stale, and I am weary of it." He beats the jailer, who yells for help.

Exton and at least two followers, all armed, come pounding in. Richard immediately understands his danger. He seizes an axe out of the hands of one of the men and promptly kills the fellow with it. He then turns on the other follower and kills him, but in so doing he exposes himself to Exton, who gives him a mortal blow. Richard, dying on the flagstones of his cell, tells Exton his murderous hand will burn in Hell, for that murderous hand has stained England with royal blood.

> **COMMENT:** Even in this moment of Richard's private suffering, it is important to the theme of the play to emphasize that England is also suffering. There is in this reference a hint, too, of the troubles that will beset the Lancaster kings because this stain on England will remain and will remind all of the circumstances in which they got their royal power.

Richard dies quickly. His last words are a prayer that his soul mount upward even as his body collapses on the cold floor.

Exton can't help paying the dead man a tribute. Richard, he says, was as full of valor as of royal blood. He hopes he has done the right thing, but he has some misgiving. "For now the Devil, that told me I did well, / Says that this deed is chronicled in Hell." But, at any rate, he will bring Richard's body to Bolingbroke. The other two who lie dead nearby shall be buried at Pomfret.

SUMMARY. This scene is Richard's.

*Horse of one of the admired, spirited breeds produced in the Arabic world, brown or brownish red in color.

1) In it he attains the nobility of character we saw him beginning to develop in an earlier episode. It is ironic that Richard the man grows really noble only after he is completely shorn of the appearances of nobility.

2) His character improvement is not artificial or incredible in the sense that Shakespeare radically changes his personality. He remains, as his long soliloquy shows, fanciful and artistically sensitive. He remains, to some extent, vacillating; he is still not sure whether it is better to be king or subject. He remains very talkative and a little petty.

3) But he *has* grown as the result of his experiences.

a. Most important, he now sees himself clearly. "I wasted time." "I bear a burden like an ass." He sees his own guilt and shortcomings.

b. He also sees others more sympathetically and now recognizes real kindness and love.

4) Though so ineffectual in handling the challenges of kingship and rather moping in his personality even in this final stage, Richard is no coward and certainly no physical weakling. Unarmed at first, he tricks and destroys two of his armed assailants before the third can injure him. His murderer's tribute is the best testimony to his bravery.

5) Psychologically, Exton's misgivings are important in our final assessment of Richard and his role in life. We are not allowed to sink back into any easy assumption that Richard deserved his death.

Act V: Scene 6

Preceded by a ceremonial flourish of trumpets, King Henry enters attended by York and other noblemen. The King remarks to York that late reports indicate that the rebels have burnt the town of Cicester (pronounced Si' sis ter; Cirencester in western England). But he has not yet had report about the fate of the rebels themselves. He turns from York to greet the entering Northumberland. Northumberland has encountered and overcome four of the chief insurgents, the Lords Oxford, Salisbury, Blunt, and Kent. He has beheaded them, and their heads are now on the way to London. Bolingbroke thanks Northumberland and promises him a reward for his diligence. Lord Fitzwater strides in. Two more rebels fell into his hands, and their heads have met the same unhappy fate. Hard on the heels of Fitzwater comes young Percy. He has captured the Bishop of Carlisle and has brought the prelate with him. He reports the death, whether from natural causes or by execution is not clear, of the archconspirator, the Abbot of Westminster. But at least he has the Bishop "to abide thy kingly doom [judgement]." The doom that Bolingbroke pronounces for Carlisle is that the Bishop should select some suitable but secluded residence. There he should live in quiet comfort. So long as he lives peaceably, he will not be disturbed. It is true, says Bolingbroke, that Carlisle has always been his enemy. Nevertheless, he admires and respects the churchman for the "high sparks of honor" he has seen in him.

RICHARD II

Exton enters. Several men follow him bearing the burden of a coffin. Exton tells Bolingbroke that he brings King Henry's "buried fear." In the coffin lies Richard of Bordeaux, "mightiest of thy greatest enemies, . . . by me hither brought." Bolingbroke, with his customary rapid adjustment to surprise and rapid power of decision, turns on Exton. "I thank thee not, for thou hast wrought / A deed of slander." The offense, as Bolingbroke sees it, is not to Richard but to Bolingbroke himself and "all this famous land." Exton protests that he thought Bolingbroke said that he wanted Richard disposed of. Bolingbroke admits that he did wish Richard dead; but that does not prevent him from despising Exton, just as the poisoner can loathe the poison. "I hate the murderer, love him [Richard] murdered." He will give Exton no reward nor sign of favor. Rather let him roam in dark and nameless obscurity, blood brother to Cain. Bolingbroke tells the nobles around him that he is saddened that his rise to power was attended by the shedding of Richard's blood. He asks them to lament with him and to put on mourning clothes. He also announces his intention of making a pilgrimage to the Holy Land "to wash this blood off from my guilty hand." All depart from our sight, following in solemn procession the "untimely bier."

COMMENT: Bolingbroke's vow to make atonement for Richard's murder by a pilgrimage to the Holy Land is never fulfilled; yet, he seems to have been entirely sincere about this. At the beginning of *Henry IV, Part 1* (Act 1, Scene 1), he refers to his disappointment because he has to postpone the fulfillment of the vow. In *Part 2* of that play (Act 3, Scene 1), he reminds his barons that he eager to conclude his wars so that he can make his promised pilgrimage. Again, as he is dying at the end of *Part 2* (Act 4, Scene 5), his mind runs on the vow he has never been able to fulfill.

SUMMARY. In this short, final scene Shakespeare presents for our sober assessment the results of the power contest that we have watched.

1) England now has a king with administrative powers.

a. Bolingbroke has in very short order suppressed the revolt against him.

b. He has also, for the time being, the energetic, positive cooperation of a group of capable men, doers like himself. This group includes the Earl of Northumberland, Henry Percy, Lord Fitzwater.

2) England has also a king who can, on occasion, withhold the mailed fist of authority and yet not endanger his power.

a. Bolingbroke knows how and when to temper his rule with mercy.

b. He is big enough himself to recognize value and worth in others. Bolingbroke shows both these qualities in his treatment of the Bishop of Carlisle.

But:

3) England has gained this king in a dubious fashion.

a. He acquired the throne by tactics dangerously close to brute force.

b. He displaced an anointed king (a point of considerable weight to an Elizabethan audience).

c. He has ensured his permanence on the throne by provoking the murder of his predecessor Richard. This act is all the more sinister because Bolingbroke himself hates it and its executor, as he makes clear to Exton.

d. He has compromised also the integrity and conscience of men like York, Aumerle, Bagot.

4) The murdered Richard, for all his faults, is a sympathetic character. In one sense he is the protagonist of the tragedy (the unsuccessful contender against evil). We find it easier to feel that he had a raw deal than to exult in the cold, political Bolingbroke's victory, despite Bolingbroke's manifest abilities.

5) England herself has been injured. Participants on both sides of this conflict have emphasized their love of England. It is not hard to believe that many of them were motivated, at least in part, by patriotism. But one ironic result of their actions has been to inflict on England a wound that will throb and fester for several generations and reigns. It will not heal until it has been through the terrible, scarifying surgery of a civil war, the Wars of the Roses (1455-1485). Both Richard and Bolingbroke bear responsibility for the political impasse that produces this tragic event. This injury to England is probably, in Shakespeare's mind, the real tragedy of the play, the most disastrous triumph of evil in the drama.

CHARACTER ANALYSES

KING RICHARD: Richard is a man who was called by an unkind fate to play a role in life for which he is not suited. He is forced to be a king, and king in a period when kings had far greater power and therefore greater responsibility than do most monarchs today. His office demands that he be authoritative, one who can command respect; that he be far-seeing and prudent in his decisions; that he be aware of and, seemingly at least, considerate of his subjects' wishes; that he be a good judge of character and able to attract men of ability as his assistants; that he be a real leader to his people—a stern figure, perhaps, but noble, just, and forceful, an emblem of security. Poor Richard is certainly lacking in most of these regal qualities. At the very beginning of the play we find both Bolingbroke and Mowbray flouting his desire that they resolve their quarrel peacefully. Far from commanding their respect, he has to bow to their wish. He has for some time been maintaining an extravagant court and at the same time draining his people by excessive taxation and arbitrary seizure of their resources. He pursues this imprudent policy despite ominous public dissatisfaction and even goes to the dangerous length of dispossessing his rival, Bolingbroke. He is so poor a judge of character that he not only unnecessarily antagonizes the ambitious Bolingbroke, who is just looking for an excuse to take over the government, but he also foolishly entrusts the reins of government, during his absense in Ireland, to his uncle, the emotional, politically inept York. York may be kindly and peace-loving, but he is obviously not the man to pick to be the King's representative. As the numerous defections prove, Richard had not inspired in the nobles any confidence in his leadership. They turn eagerly to Bolingbroke. Over Bolingbroke lies the sinister shadow of rebellion and usurpation, a distinct disadvantage; but the nobles choose his leadership in preference to Richard's legitimate reign. Bushy and Bagot agree that Richard has also lost the support of the commoners, and we find that easy to believe in view of the enthusiastic roadside turnout of well-wishers when Bolingbroke rode away to exile. Richard's belief in the Divine Right of Kings is a great liability to him. It gives him a false sense of security; for he believes that since he is the consecrated king, God will champion him against all enemies. He emphasizes the prestige and privileges this theory gave to the monarch, but he ignores the heavy responsibility it laid on the man who was chosen to represent God in secular society.

Richard was not made to be a king. But he was made, perhaps, to play at being King. He has a strong dramatic flair that makes him assume for brief periods and with real style various kingly postures. For instance, he must have timed his abrupt termination of the single combat at Coventry for its theatrical effect. Apparently he and his Council had agreed in advance on the exile sentences. He might have announced them when he first arrived at the combat ground; but why waste such a splendid opportunity for pomp and pageantry, climaxed by a sudden dramatic scene in which the king could play the featured role? The actor in him allowed him to "enjoy" his troubles as well as his triumphs. He shows this as he descends to Bolingbroke in the "base court" at Flint Castle and also in his abdication speeches at Westminster. This self-dramatizing was, unfortunately, a kind of escape from his troubles. If he had not had that outlet, he might have been forced to confront his own inadequacies more honestly. Richard had character inadequacies apart from the lack of kingly qualities. He could be petty and selfish. He shows this most clearly in his hopeful anticipation of Gaunt's death. Another aspect of this selfishness is his tendency to self-pity. This is shown in brief passages ("There I'll pine away. / A King woe's slave, shall kingly woe obey." "Alack the heavy day, / That I have worn too many winters out." "I am sworn brother . . . to grim Necessity,") and also in long speeches like his address to the English earth upon his return from Ireland and his abdication speech beginning "Aye, no—no, aye." He is unscrupulous. His excessive taxation of his people is not only politically inexpedient but it is morally wrong. But Richard tosses aside the moral warning of York on this score with a flip "Think what you will!" He lacks stability. He vacillates at all the crisis points of his career in the play: in his treatment of Bolingbroke and Mowbray; upon his arrival back from Ireland; in his reaction to Bolingbroke's demands at Flint Castle; in Westminster Hall; in his prison cell. It is true that this vacillation often arises from his rather clever analysis of all aspects of his situation; but the cleverness produces a sort of stalemate or infirmity of purpose, a failure to get things done—his major character drawback when compared to Bolingbroke.

The weaknesses of Richard are most apparent in the first half of the play. As he declines from prosperity to adversity, he becomes a more sympathetic character. We feel increasing pity for him as he incurs the series of disasters that culminate in his harsh imprisonment. The worst aspect of that imprisonment in his feeling of rejection by "this all-hating world." But, in addition to pity, we also have more cause for admiration. His recognition of the fact that Bolingbroke really can be the better ruler may be defeatist but it is also realistic. Although there is no major alteration in his personality and the self-dramatizing persists, he does accept his reverses with a kind of gentle dignity that shows some character development under the stress of misfortune. There is also development in his insight into life and human relations when, in his last hour, he feels gratitude for a small awkward gesture of love—the poorly played music. This is a different, wiser Richard than the man who had so little charity for the sick Gaunt. Of course, his final spirited resistance to his murderers assures us that, although he may have been a fatalist, he never was a coward.

Throughout the play his intellectual and artistic gifts are apparent, but they are more impressive in the final acts. Here they do not interfere, as they do earlier, with performance of his official duties. His quick, analytic mind, his fertile imagination, and his fluency of speech are ornaments to the man Richard; they are not always used well by the King Richard.

Richard is a tragic figure. His tragedy has two causes: one external and one internal. The external cause is the character of Bolingbroke, his undoubted political superiority coupled with his driving ambition. The internal and more influential cause is Richard's own character. As we have seen, his defects and gifts combine to make him a failure as a king. He is one of Shakespeare's first attempts to show that character is fate. To a large extent he caused his own tragedy.

Richard may be seen as an early Hamlet. They are both sensitive, artistic intellectuals, placed in positions that demand energetic and decisive men of action. They both analyze (are given to "thinking too precisely on the event"); they both vacillate; they both fail to meet the demands imposed upon them. Hamlet is, of course, a far more complex, far more cleverly conveived character. Some critics feel that Richard and Hamlet are sketches of what Shakespeare saw when he looked into his mirror, that they are the closest he ever came to autobiographical characterization.

BOLINGBROKE: Approximately the same age as Richard (they are both in their early thirties) and like Richard the grandson of the preceding King, Edward III, Henry, Duke of Hereford, surnamed Bolingbroke from his place of birth, is an excellent foil character to the King.

They are very different in their personalities: Richard is complicated, artistically gifted, emotional, and impulsive; Bolingbroke is comparatively simple, a man of affairs, deliberate, efficient. Bolingbroke has both the ability and the desire to rule. His strong, energetic disposition has a natural magnetism that attracts followers, both powerful men like Northumberland and York, and the humble common people. A shrewd politician, he exploits the advantage his personality gives him, as we see in his affability to the people who gather around him as he goes into exile. He is a realist who knows that effective power has little to do with the royal ceremonies and trappings in which Richard delights. He knows that it really consists in imposing one's will on others. This he does repeatedly. For instance, with Mowbray, he makes Richard agree to the Coventry combat; he forces Richard to reverse himself, makes him revoke the exile sentence and restore the Lancaster property; he quashes, in short order, the rebellion led by the Abbot of Westminster. He is a man of action who sees what is to be done and sets about doing it. Of course, he is very lucky to have Richard for a rival. Compared to such a sorry (politically speaking) figure, he was almost bound to be a success.

He plays the politician's game almost without scruples. He does not hesitate to foment civil insurrection. Even the charge of usurpation does not disturb him as he advances steadily toward the throne that he covets. He mistreats the imprisoned Richard and apparently did drop the hints that brought the murderers to Pomfret. But he is no ogre. He can be gracious, as we see in his kindness to the distraught Duchess of York; he loves his own son and was himself a good son to John of Gaunt; he feels his responsibility in Richard's death and plans to do penance for it. Like many public men before and after him, he operates on a double standard of morality—one for political life and one for his private life. He expresses this well himself in his final speech: "Though I did wish him [Richard] dead, / I hate the murderer, love him murdered."

Although so unlike, Richard and Bolingbroke are for most readers and probably for Shakespeare about equally sympathetic as characters. Each had value, but neither was really a good king for England. Richard had the legal right but not the ability; Bolingbroke had the ability but not the full legal sanction. The whole point of Shakespeare's chronicle plays is that although Bolingbroke's violation of right procedure brought England better government in his day, in the end it reduced England to a civil war and brought her to the verge of anarchy.

JOHN OF GAUNT: Gaunt appears only in the early part of the play. He dies in the first scene of the second act. Nevertheless, he is an outstanding character. First of all, he is a mouthpiece for an important aspect of the play's political philosophy. The basic political problem posed by the play is "What can be done about an incompetent king?" Gaunt is solid as a rock in his position that the King may be reproved but not removed or violently attacked. He himself reproves Richard more scathingly than any other character in the play: "Thou liest in reputation sick," "Thou . . .

Commit'st thy anointed body to the cure / Of these physicians who first wounded thee," "Landlord of England art thou now, not King." "Live in thy shame." But he will not "lift an angry arm against His [God's] minister." To Gaunt, the King is God's deputy. God ordained him for that office, and only God can remove or punish him. He is well aware that some kings betray their divine election; he has had to live for some time with frightening evidence of that fact of life. Nevertheless, the theory of the Divine Right of Kings seems to him to give stability to society; he abides by it steadfastly.

Gaunt, however, is not just a personified political slogan. In his few appearances he becomes a flesh and blood man with a serious but rather attractive personality. What we notice about him particularly is that he seems stable but not rigid. He is firm in his disapproval of much that Richard has been doing, but he can cooperate with the King. In the first scene he not only brings Bolingbroke to court in response to Richard's request, but he also tries, as Richard asks him to, to get Bolingbroke to withdraw his challenge of Mowbray. He is willing to listen for some time to the "exclaims" of the widowed Duchess of Gloucester. He gives her this kind of courtesy and opportunity for emotional release. But he does not compromise his conviction that Richard must be left to God's judgement. He is consistent in this attitude toward the King even when Richard's policy touches him very closely. So, as a Council member, he supports the exile sentence for his son. But he is also a father, and he sees no reason to hide his personal grief at the sentence. The love for his son that causes this grief also gives him the strength to surmount it in order to cheer up the departing Bolingbroke.

His great moment in the play comes in his last scene. In it we see how superior he is to the King who calls him a "lunatic lean-witted fool." What Richard is pleased to call lunacy seems to us to be genuine, eloquent love of England and a sensible fear of Richard's shady financial policies. Gaunt is angry and forceful in his final speech. Neither the weakness of mortal illness nor the petty cruelty of Richard daunts his strong spirit. He has our admiration as he leaves the play and life.

EDMUND, DUKE OF YORK: York resembles his nephew Richard more than he does his brother John of Gaunt. He is an emotional and, in some ways, weak old man. He has convictions, but his defense of them is usually feeble. This inadequacy makes him increasingly cautious and apprehensive. Throughout the play York seems pursued by fears. His first speeches, in a conversation with Gaunt, show that he agrees with his brother about Richard's rule, but, unlike Gaunt, he fears to rile Richard. When rebellion breaks out in the land that he as Lord Governor is responsible for, fear almost unmans him. The discovery of his son's treachery against Henry IV puts him in a state of panic.

But he can overcome his fears and speak out as boldly as Gaunt himself. When Richard seizes Bolingbroke's property, York is really aroused; he gives the King a tongue lashing as harsh as Gaunt's earlier denunciation of Richard. He is almost as wrathful with Bolingbroke when that nephew alarms the realm with rebellion. As he himself complains, he is caught in the middle between these two difficult nephews. He is conscious of his family responsibility to them and tries, sporadically, to fill their dead fathers' shoes. But these plain-speaking periods are brief, and anyway his criticism is largely ignored. Usually he handles both the younger men with tearful caution.

His treatment of his own erring son is peculiar. He deserts him as he never deserted Bolingbroke or even Richard. With his capitulation to Bolingbroke, his character seems to deteriorate; and his natural fearfulness becomes acute, base and very selfish, to the extent that he could sacrifice his own son.

York appears to be a well-intentioned, perhaps even gentle man whose worst characteristics are emphasized by the sad events of this plot.

DUKE OF AUMERLE: Although he appears frequently in the play, this character is not well developed. He has very little to say, and, until the end, does very little. He is usually in Richard's company but does not seem to be deeply committed to Richard's cause. It is true that he is one of the small band of nobles who are with Richard in Wales. It is also true that he joins the conspiracy against Bolingbroke. But he is unnaturally cool and detached in these exciting situations, improbably so for a man caught in a political and family crisis.

By this detachment Shakespeare may be trying to suggest that Aumerle is the opportunistic type of follower who has no real loyalties. He really cares little which of his rival cousins he serves. Early in the play he seems to favor Bolingbroke; he asks Bolingbroke to write him from exile and rides away with this cousin on the road that will take him out of England. At the play's end he is glad to submit to Bolingbroke. It is also possible that Aumerle is so colorless and almost faceless simply because Shakespeare did not take sufficient care with this character and was content to leave him only partly sketched.

But Aumerle does come alive in the York family scene in the final act. Even here he does not have the vitality and conviction of his father and mother; but he is human in his attempt to hide the incriminating document from his father and in his frightened, breathless petition to King Henry.

THOMAS MOWBRAY, DUKE OF NORFOLK: The primary function of this character is to provide early in the play a situation that will bring out the aggressiveness and boldness of Bolingbroke and the weaknesses of Richard. He performs this service admirably. His own belligerence sparks Bolingbroke's mettle. Richard can't control either of them. In his harsh exile sentence he shows toward Mowbray the same rash arbitrariness of a weak man that he shows in seizing the Lancaster property.

But, in addition to his usefulness in revealing aspects of the two main characters, Mowbray is sufficiently well developed to be interesting in himself. Of course, the chief cause of our interest in him is that we are never sure about his guilt in the death of Gloucester. If he was implicated, and it seems likely that he was since Bolingbroke dares to "appeal" him, he evidently acted as the King's agent. Richard's speech to Mowbray just before the Coventry combat is due to begin may mean that he has a special reliance on Mowbray. "Securely [confidently] I espy / Virtue with valor couched in thine eye." Also, Mowbray's obviously hurt reaction to his "heavy sentence" which he says is "all unlooked for from your Highness' mouth", could indicate some understanding between Richard and this nobleman. If this is true, Mowbray could well feel that Richard had violated their understanding.

Even if we believe him guilty of this political murder (or of facilitating it), we find Mowbray a rather sympathetic as well as complex character. His differing reactions to the two types of attack on him are interesting and convincing. He is brave and resourceful in facing Bolingbroke's accusations; he does not yield an inch to this type of attack. But to Richard's banishment edict he offers no resistance, although he considers it unjust. He shows that he is as much a Divine Right of Kings man as is Gaunt. The last reference to him is Carlisle's report of his death in Venice. It is a tribute to him as a soldier. Carlisle praises him as a crusader who had fought against pagans, Turks, and Saracens. In his death he gave "his pure soul unto his captain Christ / Under whose colors he had fought so long." This tribute comes from a character whose integrity we have reason to respect. Therefore Mowbray makes a fairly honorable exit from the play.

EARL OF NORTHUMBERLAND: Bearing the same name (Henry Percy) as his son, he is chief of the powerful Percy family of Northern England. He is well suited to the position, at least in the sense that he can assume and discharge responsibilities. He is able to think for himself, and he is courageous. He showed these qualities in his decision to abandon Richard's cause and ally himself with Bolingbroke when the latter was expected at Ravenspurgh. But his repeated "haugh [haughty] and insulting" coldness to Richard makes him seem a bully. Our natural aversion to him is intensified by Richard's prophecy that eventually Bolingbroke also will have reason to hate him. But in the time span of this play he serves Bolingbroke well, in a blunt, soldierly fashion. He brings to Bolingbroke's support both his brother, Thomas Percy, Earl of Worcester, and his heir, young Harry Percy (Hotspur-to-be). On the whole, he is a rather flat, one-dimensional character, useful in the plot but lacking humanizing development.

SIR PIERCE OF EXTON: Sir Pierce (Peter) is another follower of Bolingbroke, and he says he is the new King's friend. His actual role in the tragedy, however, is that of Richard's Nemesis (goddess of punishment). Richard must pay physically for his mistakes, and Sir Pierce extracts that payment. It is a thankless, forbidding role, and Exton is conscienceless and brutal in his execution of it. But Shakespeare avoids creating a monster. Exton is human. He is rather weakly and stupidly human in his deliberation before setting out to Pomfret to do the murder. His immediate reactions after the murder, his praise of Richard, and his wave of guilt, are those of a simple, impulsive man who leaps before he really looks. All Exton's powers of foresight were probably concentrated on pleasing King Henry. He does please him, but not with the beneficial results to himself that he anticipates. Although more sinister and ignoble than Mowbray, he shares with Richard's hapless follower the usual fate of those who do a monarch's dirty work—ruthless rejection.

THE BISHOP OF CARLISLE: The Bishop is just the opposite of the opportunistic and conscienceless Exton. He is involved in politics as were most of the high churchmen of England in his day; but he is not the creature of any politician, not even of the King, be he Richard or Henry. He admonishes Richard in fatherly fashion and urges him to settle down to a real campaign against the rebel army of Bolingbroke. His treatment at this time of Richard may be gentle, but he makes his opposition to Richard's fecklessness clear. With Bolingbroke and his party he is far from gentle. He tells them emphatically that they are doing wrong and that harm will come of it. His fearlessness is rewarded with arrest but probably also with the peace of mind an easy conscience affords. Pleasurable moments are rare in this sad play, but we do enjoy one at the end when King Henry, instead of destroying his enemy Carlisle, shows respect and admiration for this honorable and valiant antagonist.

BUSHY, GREEN, BAGOT: We see these three minor noblemen as intimates of both Richard and his Queen. Although not exactly alike in their relationship to King Richard, all three agree in what they reveal about the King. This illumination of the character of Richard is their chief function in the play. If the hint of their moral depravity in Act 3, Scene 1, is to be credited (and most critics are doubtful that it should be), his association with them taints the character of Richard. They certainly show that he relied too much on favorites who may have shared his artistic and intellectual interests but who had nothing to contribute to the political strength of his rule. He entrusted to them political and military responsibilities, but when the crisis came they deserted these responsibilities. Bushy and Green do remain loyal to Richard and die his men. But, since everyone at Bristol Castle was executed when it was captured by Bolingbroke, they may not have had much choice. Bagot, in some undisclosed circumstances, did have a choice and chose to go over to Bolingbroke. We find him strenuously identifying with the Bolingbroke party in the accusation of Aumerle as Gloucester's murderer. After that we hear no more of him. Presumably he found a niche for himself in Henry's court and put from his mind the old days and friendships.

THE WOMEN IN THE PLAY: None of the women in the play has a major part. This is a tragedy rooted in politics, and in the 1300's politics was definitely a man's world. Three women, however, do have roles of some importance. Each of these women is a distinctive character.

The Queen is the most prominent of the three. She is a gentle young woman whose bitter experiences in the play, temporarily anyway, alter her personality for the worse. Her very first speech, one of kind inquiry for Gaunt's health, shows her loving nature. This sensitivity makes her grieve deeply for the absent Richard, but her innate passiveness keeps her from doing much about the causes of her grief. Her husband's absence continues, and she waits, without news and full of apprehensions, in the country, at Langley. It is not strange that she speaks so crossly to the inoffensive gardener. Her sweet, mild disposition has grown sour with fear. In her final meeting with Richard, she is still frightened and rather irritable at first, but more than that she is wifely. She is shocked by her husband's ravaged looks; she tries to stimulate him to help himself; she asks to share his imprisonment; and, most important of all, she tries to tell him that he is loved. Dramatically, the Queen is a sort of reflection or restatement of Richard. Like his, her experience in the play is very sad. She is indeed "a weeping Queen."

The Duchess of Gloucester is also a weeping lady, but there is more indignation and fight in her grief than in the Queen's. She seeks satisfaction in revenge; but, on the other hand, she is no virago, for she accepts quietly enough Gaunt's reason for not actively revenging his brother. Of course, she makes clear that she certainly does not agree with Gaunt. One of her functions is to give Gaunt an opportunity to air his suspicions of Richard's complicity in Gloucester's murder and also to voice his Divine Right of Kings code. Her final speeches stress her loneliness. Her husband is gone; her home is empty and cold, unwarmed even by the satisfaction of vengeance properly meted out; she discourages York from visiting her; and Gaunt is too distracted by his own concerns to realize how very alone she is. She says she is going home to die, and her death is reported not long afterwards. She has, as Gaunt advised, taken her complaint to the Champion of Widows. Even in her death she is lonely, for York (and presumably others) is prevented by the emergency of the rebellion from going to pay her his last respects. She, like the Queen, adds to the tragedy the poignancy of innocent suffering.

The Duchess of York, although also involved in the tragic events, differs from the other two women because she is more fortunate and because she unintentionally provides us with a few laughs. She is much more energetic and determined than the Queen or her sister-in-law. She is much less intimidated by the men and their politics. Although excitable, she is able to think clearly in an emergency. It is she, not Aumerle, who has the excellent idea that he must outride his father and get to King Henry first. She sees that she also can be useful in the interview with the King and wastes no time getting to court. She selects the strategy that she feels Henry will succumb to, and she persists. We feel that she deserves her success. It is true that she cuts a rather ludicrous figure in her agitation and single-mindedness, but she is really not as ludicrous as her senile old husband who tries to dismiss her as foolish.

These three women contribute little to the plot of this tragedy, but they add great emotional depth and enrichment. They show us how political policy can work out in terms of human sorrows, struggles and triumphs. With the exception of Richard, they are the greatest contributors of feeling to this drama.

MINOR CHARACTERS: There are many minor characters in this play. Most of them are courtiers, adherents of Richard or Bolingbroke. Their character expression is pretty well limited to their display of political partisanship on one side or the other. For example, the Earl of Salisbury, Lord Berkeley, Sir Stephen Scroop, and the Abbot of Westminster play this type of part for the Richard faction. Lord Ross, Lord Willoughby, Lord Fitzwater, and the young Harry Percy are their opposite numbers in the Bolingbroke party.

Of the remaining minor characters, two are of especial interest. Both are commoners and of too humble a rank to play any political role. One is the gardener at Langley. He is memorable because of the garden allegory that he relates as he rids his garden of weeds and also because of his treatment of the Queen. He is honest and forthright with her, though somewhat unfeeling, perhaps, in his abrupt disclosure of Richard's reverses. But he makes up for this bluntness by the pity with which he regards the departing Queen—a pity that is tolerant even of her waspish attack on him.

The other character has an even briefer part. He is the groom who comes to visit Richard. He is a simple man and not very tactful in his choice of subjects for conversation, but good-hearted and kind. Dramatically, he contrasts in many ways with the murderers who follow him into the cell. Most poignant of these contrasts is the juxtaposition of powerless good and powerful evil.

CRITICAL COMMENTARY

CONTEMPORARY REACTION. If public reaction be considered a species of criticism, probably *Richard II* had the most spectacular initial criticism of any of Shakespeare's plays. When it was first produced in 1595, or soon thereafter, it was considered sensationally and dangerously topical. This was the period of the on-and-off quarreling between Queen Elizabeth I and her erstwhile favorite, the Earl of Essex. Essex began to charge that Elizabeth's rule was deteriorating because she had surrounded herself with untrustworthy advisors. She, on the other hand, suspected that the rash Essex was jealous of those advisors and that he wanted to control her, if not actually seize her throne. The parallels between this situation and the plot of *Richard II* were obvious, painfully so to Elizabeth herself. She is reported to have been displeased by the play's popularity and to have said in some indignation, "I am Richard II, know you not that?" Essex was seen by his sympathizers as a second Bolingbroke, competent and efficient, and a very desirable replacement for the supposedly weakening Elizabeth. This topicality doubtlessly accounts for the unusual success of the play in the late 1590's. It probably accounts also for the censor's scrissoring of it when it was first printed in 1597 and 1598. In these early editions the Westminster Hall deposition scene is omitted entirely. Elizabeth or her officials considered it too inflammatory. In February, 1601, Essex made a desperate, foolhardy attempt to oust Elizabeth's council and to re-instate himself as her chief advisor. Shakespeare's Globe company of actors was hired to do a special performance on the eve of this attempt. The intention was to use the play as a propaganda weapon for Essex's cause and as a firebrand to ignite the emotions of the men who would take part in the next day's uprising. When approached, the Lord Chamberlain's Men (the Globe company) were not eager to do this special performance. Their objection apparently was not to the political danger of angering Elizabeth but to the fact that the play was now "old" and would attract a small audience. They agreed to do it, however, when Essex's representatives offered to add forty shillings to the box-office receipts. The insurrection on the following day, Sunday, February 8, was a miserable failure. As a result of it, the colorful but careless Essex was beheaded on February 24, at the age of thirty-three, and a number of his followers were also executed or imprisoned. The Globe actors were very lucky. They were interrogated but were released, and no charges were made against them. Perhaps the fact that they were Elizabeth's favorite acting company helped them.

This connection with the Elizabethan political situation still has considerable interest for people who study the play. But most critics who have written about *Richard II* have been more interested in two other subjects: the character of Richard and the place of the play in the evolution of Shakespeare's dramatic skill. Various critical opinions about these two subjects are now presented.

EARLIER CRITICS CONCERNING CHARACTER OF RICHARD. There is general unanimity among critics that Richard's character was weak or at least weak in the qualities demanded of a ruler. Many, however, see him as artistically gifted. Samuel Johnson, one of the earliest and most thoughtful of Shakesperian critics, said, in the notes that he provided for his edition of the play, that Shakespeare apparently intended "to raise Richard to esteem in his fall, and consequently to interest the reader in his favour." But Johnson, who was extremely unlike Richard in his temperament and ideals, could not find Richard very admirable at any time in the play. He is especially offended by Richard's failure to be kingly. He finds in him only "passive fortitude, the virtue of a confessor rather than of a king," and he speaks later of his "childish prattle." He does feel, though, that this hero who is "imperious and oppressive" at the play's beginning learns from distress to be "wise, patient, and pious."

William Hazlitt and Samuel T. Coleridge were men of another age and had critical standards rather different from Johnson's. But they agree with the earlier critic in their estimate of Richard. However, since they are critics of the Romantic Period (early nineteenth century) and therefore interested in the audience's emotional reaction to the hero, they also stress the pity that Richard arouses. Hazlitt reviews Richard's character in this way: "After the first act, in which the arbitrariness of his behaviour only proves his want of resolution, we see him staggering under the unlooked-for blows of fortune, bewailing his loss of kingly power, not preventing it, sinking under the aspiring genius of Bolingbroke, his authority trampled on, his hopes failing him, and his pride crushed and broken down under insults and injuries, which his own misconduct had provoked, but which he had not courage or manliness to resent." But he does find the King a sympathetic character in one way. "We feel neither respect nor love for the deposed monarch; for he is as wanting in energy as in principle: but we pity him. . . . He is human in his distresses; for to feel pain, and sorrow, weaknesses, disappointment, remorse and anguish is the lot of humanity. . . . The sufferings of the man make us forget that he ever was a king." Coleridge, in his Shakespearean lectures, criticizes Richard for his womanish weakness, his relish for flattery, his "hard usage of his friends," and his irresolution. But he, too, pities Richard. He reminds us that Richard was well loved by two admirable people, the Queen and the Bishop of Carlisle, and that this should recommend him to us. "We cannot, therefore, help pitying and wishing he had been placed in a rank where he would have been less exposed, and where he might have been happy and useful." Coleridge is one of the first to stress Richard's intellectual acuteness and his powers of poetic expression. "Were there an actor capable of representing Richard, the part would delight us more than any other of Shakespeare's masterpieces—with, perhaps, the single exception of King Lear."

LATER CRITICS CONCERNING CHARACTER OF RICHARD: Most of the critics of the late nineteenth century and the twentieth have agreed with Johnson, Coleridge, and Hazlitt in stressing Richard's weakness. If, like Coleridge and Hazlitt, they have contributed a new viewpoint to the criticism of Richard's character, it has probably been their emphasis on Richard's artistic personality and the problems it presents for him. Edward Dowden, one of the most eminent of the Victorian critics, thought that Richard's temperament made an actor of him in every situation, that all life was a show for him, and neither calamity nor prosperity truly real. A. C. Bradley, to many the greatest of all students of Shakespeare's tragedies, explores the similarities between Richard, Hamlet, and Shakespeare himself. Richard, he says in his *Shakespearean Tragedy*, "may, like . . . Hamlet, have owed his existence in part to Shakespeare's personal familiarity with the weaknesses and dangers of the imaginative temperament." Others comment on Richard's "incomparable imagination," and command of "exquisite images," his "aesthetic pleasure in his own disgrace," "his kingly graces," "his brilliant fancy," and "beautiful tangles of . . . arabesque wit." Most of them consider Richard's artistic sensitivity and eloquence attractive features of his personality; and most think that Shakespeare also considered them attractive. But most think too, that Shakespeare intends to show Richard as faulty and guilty of misgovernment. As J.A.R. Marriott expresses it, "his citadel was betrayed from within." Some do contend that Shakespeare handles this business of making Richard admirable and guilty and pitiful rather awkwardly. Shakespeare, they feel, may have and probably did admire Richard the man, may even have identified with him as a fellow-artist, but did not admire him as a ruler, saw him as villain-like in that role. As Elmer E. Stoll puts it in his *Shakespeare Studies*, it is hard to believe that Shakespeare meant that failure as a Richard is better than success as a Henry.

But there is a dissenting voice here. It is an important one and authoritative because it is the voice of a distinguished poet as well as critic. It is the voice of William Butler Yeats. Yeats seems to believe that Shakespeare considered the imaginative Richard superior in all respects and in all situations to the realistic and competent Bolingbroke. "I cannot believe that Shakespeare looked on his Richard II with other than sympathetic eyes, understanding indeed how ill-fitted he was to be King, at a certain moment of history, but understanding that he was lovable and full of capricious fancy, ... He made his King fail, a little because he lacked some qualities that were doubtless common among his scullions, but more because he had certain qualities that are uncommon in all ages. To suppose that Shakespeare preferred the man who deposed his King is to suppose that Shakespeare judged men with the eyes of a Municipal Councillor weighing the merits of a Town Clerk. . . . He saw, indeed, as I think, in Richard II the defeat that awaits all, whether they be Artist or Saint, who find themselves where men ask of them a rough energy and have nothing to give but some contemplative virtue, whether lyrical phantasy, or sweetness of temper, or dreamy dignity, or love of God, or love of His creatures."

CONCERNING SHAKESPEARE'S DRAMATIC DEVELOPMENT. The other subject that has interested evaluators is the stage of the author's evolution represented by the play. Written about 1595, it belong probably at the beginning of what is sometimes called his lyrical period. He had behind him some half-dozen years of play writing, but he was still five or six years away from his most powerful plays. So this play shows a dramatist in the process of development. Among the aspects of the play that the critics have examined from this viewpoint of evolution of talent are these three: the plot, the concept of tragedy, the style.

PLOTTING. These writers have found the plot defective. Samuel Johnson, patriotic gentleman that he was, preferred the history plays to Shakespeare's other works; but he did point out that these chronicle plays were apt to be weak in plot unity. He thought that *Richard II* showed signs of revision, of an attempt to tailor historical facts and events into an artistic plot; but he considered the attempt unsuccessful. George Saintsbury, a contemporary of Dowden, is more specific. "The whole . . . handling of the play, whether we look at plot, character, diction, or versification, speaks a period at which the poet has already learned a great deal, but has not learned everything. He has already acquired the full disposition of the chronicle-play after a fashion which nobody but himself had yet shown; but he has not yet discovered the full secret of diversifying and adorning it . . . . The history . . . is still too much of a *mere* history." In the opinion of Hazelton Spencer, a more recent critic, the "whole falls between the two stools of tragedy and chronicle-history." Another modern critic, A. P. Rossiter, finds Shakespeare in difficulty with his plot especially at the beginning (which he says is too abrupt to be a good beginning) and at the end (which he complains is confusing and "ragged"). Spencer, too, considers the actual assassination weak. "The hero's violence at the end of the scene reverts to obvious theatricalism. The dramatist still has a long way to go before he is to achieve the bloody but profoundly tragic and poetic finales of *Hamlet, Othello, King Lear, Macbeth* and *Anthony and Cleopatra.*" Others agree that the plot lacks tight continuity of cause and effect from one episode to the next. Part of this plot difficulty they ascribe to Shakespeare's manipulation of our attitudes toward both Richard and Bolingbroke. He makes each play a double role, hero and villain, and this prevents a really smooth plot sequence. Another common objection is to the lack of comic relief. What there is of this is limited to the York family crisis, and not all critics find this really comic. Finally, there are a number of curious gaps in the plot. Who did kill Gloucester? Did Bolingbroke, when he first returned from exile, intend to seize the throne or just recover his lost property? What happened to Bagot? And there are other less conspicuous problems. To sum up, Shakespeare shows his comparative inexperience in his failure to produce a smoothly developing, diversified, unified plot. It is true, though, that this play is better in this regard than some of the other chronicle plays. It is also true that *Richard II* is a fine introduction to the other three plays which follow in its tetralogy, *Henry IV, Part 1* and *Part 2,* and *Henry V.*

IN CHARACTERIZATION. Character is usually more important than plot, and the critics are really more interested in what Shakespeare was able to do at this stage with a tragic hero. Bradley is decidedly negative in his verdict. To him, Richard is "scarcely a tragic character." If he is, it is "only because his fall from prosperity to adversity is so great." Richard is, he feels, only a first, very tentative step toward Shakespeare's great tragic figures. These figures are great in the sense that they are never mean or small-minded; therefore, they give an "impression of waste" in their ruin. Richard, he feels, *is* mean and petty and so does not excite the same sense of awe and regret. H. B. Charlton, in his consideration of Shakespeare's tragedies, agrees that Richard lacks the "momentousness" indispensable to the true tragic hero. But if, instead of looking ahead to the figures of Hamlet, Macbeth, Othello and Lear, the critic reviews what Shakespeare had done before 1595, his opinion is usually more favorable. Shakespeare is experimenting with the tragedy of character as distinguished from the tragedy of circumstances. Richard is doomed, in part, by external circumstances, for example Bolingbroke's ambition; but he is doomed largely by his own qualities, some actually evil and others just inappropriate for his position. Early in this century, C. H. Herford felt that Shakespeare showed progress in this play in evolving a tragedy of the individual soul in a political setting. Thomas Marc Parrott acclaims "the drift of Shakespeare's genius toward the creation of a new tragedy, the tragedy of character foredoomed to ruin." And G. B. Harrison agrees: "Richard's tragedy is not that he came to degradation, misery, and death, but that he wrought his own destruction.... Shakespeare had now begun to realize that character is fate."

IN STYLE: The style occasioned the earliest of known comments about the play by a literary critic. In 1679, John Dryden, in his preface to another Shakespearean play, praised delightedly the "passionate description" of Richard's sorry return to London as part of Bolingbroke's triumph. "I have scarce read anything comparable to it in any other language." Later critics have been as conscious as Dryden of the play's style, but most of them are somewhat less enthusiastic than Dryden. It is recognized that this is a very "poetic" play—poetic in its great use of rime, in its flowery diction, and in its imaginative and emotional emphasis. Saintsbury, a good judge of Shakespeare in this respect, emphasizes that the versification and diction are better than in the early plays, but that there is too much rime and too little prose relief and that the speeches for all their fine imagery are stiff compared to the great fluid speeches that Shakespeare would write later. E. K. Chambers finds it sufficiently lyrical to justify some kind of operatic treatment. In it, as in *Romeo and Juliet* and *Midsummer Night's Dream*, Shakespeare has his "singing robes" on. But, as Chambers points out, this is not the style for great tragedy. Shakespeare learns the deficiencies of this tragedy and goes on to the more restrained and noble style of his high tragic dramas. Harrison rejoices that this is the last of his plays in which Shakespeare "sacrificed drama to poetry." We may deduce, therefore, that, as far as style goes, we have here a play in which Shakespeare is very much the poet and not fully a dramatist. This aspect of the play, more than the plot handling or the concept of tragedy, marks him, in the opinion of the critics, as still the learner in the dramatic and theatrical world.

We may generalize the findings of these studies of *Richard II*'s place in the evolution of Shakespeare's genius in a phrase of Saintsbury's. He speaks of the work's "curious immature splendor." That phrase conveys both the admiration most critics have for the progress Shakespeare made in his apprentice years and also their recognition that the author of *Richard II* is still an experimenting writer.

CONCERNING THE IMAGERY. Caroline Spurgeon's famous study of Shakespeare's imagery is a good example of the specialized kind of criticism with which we can conclude this critical commentary. She found that there are at least four recurrent images in *Richard II*. Dominant is the plant and garden image. Its symbolism of growth and need for careful tending is very appropriate to plays tracing national development. (It's in the other chronicles, too.) In *Richard II*, we think immediately of the garden allegory that the Queen overhears. There are also briefer images. The Duchess of Gloucester calls Edward III's sons "seven fair branches springing from one root." Gaunt calls himself "a too long withered flower," and the Queen sees Richard as her "fair rose." Miss Spurgeon believes there is evidence here and in the recurrence of this type of image elsewhere in his writing that Shakespeare had a lifelong interest in gardening. Another recurrent image, as the play synopsis has emphasized, is the sun symbol for the monarch. Threatening it, antagonistic symbols of rain, snow, and other forms of water appear at times. Images connected with birth, generation, and inheritance are also conspicuous. They are appropriate in a play so concerned with family relationships and problems. Gaunt calls England "this nurse, this teeming womb of royal kings." Through the Queen's speeches when she is disturbed by her premonition of trouble to come, run several images of this type: "Some unborn sorrow, ripe in fortune's womb / Is coming towards me." This grief has no ancestry, but its hour has arrived, and Green is "the midwife to my woe." The several warnings and prophecies of impending disasters speak of the unborn children who will suffer those ills, a legacy from their sinful fathers. Richard's final long speech also uses images of begetting. His brain and soul, like two parents, "beget / A generation of still-breeding thoughts, / And these same thoughts people this little world."

Naturally, this early play has not attracted as much critical attention as the later masterpieces. But it has interested and even excited many of the best Shakespearean critics. They have found its combination of strengths and weaknesses both exasperating and instructive.

ESSAY QUESTIONS AND ANSWERS FOR REVIEW

1. Discuss the father-son relationships in the play.

Answer: Shakespeare gives us an opportunity in this play to study father-son relationships from at least five points of view. We are first aware of this theme in connection with John of Gaunt and his son Bolingbroke. Their relationship seems good. They are friendly, but each feels free to act independently. It is true that, in the opening speech of the play, Richard implies that Gaunt has "brought" his son to court to accuse Mowbray; but the word is Richard's. From what we learn later of Bolingbroke, it seems likely that he came voluntarily and not at his father's insistence. Gaunt respects his son's judgement as he immediately shows when he assures Richard that Bolingbroke has good cause for his treason charge against Mowbray. The father does not interfere at all in the long and heated discussion that follows when Bolingbroke and Mowbray appear before Richard. He is content that Bolingbroke can handle his own affairs. Not until Richard directly asks for his intervention does he speak. Then he does not attempt to argue with Bolingbroke; he merely tries to "be a make-peace" and asks his son as a gesture of obedience to relinquish Mowbray's gage. Despite the reference to obedience, this does not seem like paternal domination. Gaunt does not become angry when Bolingbroke resists him nor does he even seem surprised. He probably really admires his son's independence and does not want to challenge it. Bolingbroke also respects his father. One of his final wishes before the Coventry fight-to-the-death is that he may be a credit to his father in this combat. He feels that his own courage and skill derive from the valor of his father's character. The last conversation between this father and son occurs just after Bolingbroke hears his banishment edict. In it Gaunt shows the greater warmth and family feeling. This may be ascribed partly to Gaunt's age and his premonition of death. He feels that this is a final parting. Therefore, he rouses himself to do, this last time, his best for his son; so he does not dwell on his own grief at the separation; he tries to buoy up Bolingbroke's spirits. He extends to this son a gift that could be valuable all Bolingbroke's life, not just in this present emergency. It is the gift of a cheerful, optimistic attitude toward the future, despite present reverses. Bolingbroke is too full of his trouble and frustration to meet his father halfway; but he listens to him, and he does his father the courtesy of telling him just how he does feel in his bleak disappointment. John of Gaunt and Bolingbroke show the tensions that normally exist between father and son, but they reveal also that those tensions have not ruptured their relationship.

The situation between Aumerle and his father, the Duke of York, is quite different. Between them there seems to be a complete breakdown in communication. This may be symbolized by Aumerle's absence from home at the moment of his father's great need for support. When the word of the Bolingbroke rebellion reaches York, he sends for his son, but Aumerle is not available. The little that these two say to each other is almost entirely hostile and quarrelsome. They clash at Langley about the treasonous document the father finds on Aumerle's person. York does not wait for an explanation. Aumerle does not offer one. They go on to expose their conflict to the King himself. York's indictment of Aumerle at court seems monstrous, but Shakespeare has given us at least the negative preparation of never showing them friendly or affectionate.

More lightly sketched but also more happy is the relationship between the two Henry Percies, father and son. In the brief episode in which we see them together, they display the same ease in each other's presence that the Lancasters showed. This son is a much younger person than Bolingbroke. His father still addresses him as "boy" and rather curtly reminds him of his manners to Bolingbroke. But Harry is sure enough of his father's reasonableness to remind him, in turn, that he has never met Northumberland's powerful friend. His mannerly speech following the introduction shows him eager to imitate and support his father's political schemes. So these two, like Gaunt and Bolingbroke, seem in accord.

Slighter treatments of this father-son theme also appear in the play. In the last act Bolingbroke shifts roles and assumes the father's burdens, troubled by his reckless, willful son, who does not appear in this play. Both Bolingbroke's concern and his confidence in Prince Hal's better qualities suggest that this relationship has at least the possibility of prospering in the end. Relevant here, too, is the angered York's gibe at Richard that his father, the Black Prince, would never have treated family and country as Richard is now doing. This passage about the Black Prince reminds us that Richard knew his father for only ten years. It lends support to the feeling of some that Richard's early orphan status and lack of paternal control partly accounted for his failure as a ruler. He who would rule well must have learned to obey well.

2. Contrast Richard and Bolingbroke as political figures.

Answer: Neither Richard nor Bolingbroke is a great Shakespearean characterization; but each has considerable complexity and credibility as a human being, and they certainly are different. Shakespeare is chiefly interested in their difference as rulers. To highlight this, he places them, several times in the play, in similar political situations. For instance, our introduction to Richard occurs at a time when his political finesse is being put to a test. He is confronted with the problem of the quarrel between Mowbray and Bolingbroke. It is important that the quarreling cease, but it is more important that Richard's royal supremacy be maintained. Richard allows the situation to develop into a virtual defiance of the royal will. This occurs because he tries to prevent the judicial combat, a normal enough procedure, and tries to force the two aroused noblemen to compromise their honor by withdrawing their gages. In other words, Richard takes a position which he had a right to take as king, but which was imprudent. He should have foreseen that it would be very hard—impossible, in fact,—for him to maintain; a good administrator would have. The end of the play shows Bolingbroke in a very similar situation. The nobles are again wrangling,—and about the same issue, responsibility for Gloucester's death. But Bolingbroke handles the situation quite differently. When they have maneuvered themselves into their combat challenges, he does not interfere. Nor does he allow his authority to be challenged. Instead he takes the initiative and, even before he is asked to, says he will order a trial by combat. They should all "rest under gage / Till we assign you to your days of trial." Bolingbroke, unlike Richard, realizes that the lesser evil (judicial combat) must be tolerated to protect the greater good (the monarch's authority and the security it gives the land).

At other times they are both placed in situations that threaten their prestige and position. Richard faces defeat when he returns from Ireland. His reaction to it is to talk fancifully and at great length (mostly about how he feels), and do nothing. He also swings giddily between the heights of hope and despair, with very little basis for either extreme. At the end of the scene he is as lacking in a plan for action as he was when he started to consider his position, despite the fact that he has at hand advisors eager to counsel him. It is not that he is really indolent and not that he is a coward. It is that he is the type of person who reacts to a problem emotionally rather than attacking it by action. Bolingbroke, for his part, suffers a major reversal when Richard pronounces the exile sentences. He talks, too, but much more briefly than Richard and to his father. Officially he says almost nothing, although we know from his conversation with Gaunt that he is upset. He is controlled; he is already planning his strategy. It is a strategy of action, a strategy that he follows consistently, although he cannot at this point in the play foresee all its details. It is a strategy that will bring him home from France to Ravenspurgh; to alliance with Northumberland and the other rebels; across England to Berkeley, Bristol and "the base court" at Flint; to the welcome of the London populace; and, finally, to the throne and crown in the Hall at Westminster.

They are both placed in a situation that tests their resolution—their staying power. This is the confrontation at Flint Castle. Richard puts up a brief show of authority and determination, but it is a bubble thing that bursts when it brushes the iron of Bolingbroke's resolution. With incredible speed Richard yields his kingly responsibility and status. Bolingbroke, on the other hand, is determined to hold out for his two demands—the revoking of the exile sentence and the restoring of his property. It is true that Richard's lack of fight makes unnecessary any great show of resolution on Bolingbroke's part, but he gives every evidence of being prepared. These three situations and others that could be mentioned show how different the two first cousins are. Richard is incompetent, emotional and vacillating, irresolute. Bolingbroke is administratively competent and realistic, steady and accomplishing, tenacious of purpose. Bolingbroke is obviously a foil to Richard, a tool by which Shakespeare shows by contrast the political weaknesses of Richard. We are not surprised by the popular preference for Bolingbroke, shown in both the common people's enthusiasm for him and the nobility's defection to him. Even without the added goad of Richard's unpopular taxation policies, we would expect many people to transfer their political welfare from Richard's feeble hands to the firm grasp of Bolingbroke, if they could. E. K. Chambers has an interesting observation about the difference between these two cousins. To him, they represent the two contrasting personalities "between which, from the beginning, the inheritance of this world has been divided." They are the dreamer and the doer; the man who ponders and fancies and the man who acts. Shakespeare certainly gives the political victory to the doer, but he is not partisan. The personal victory appears to be Richard's. At least, we are sufficiently sympathetic to him to wish we could have seen him operating in a situation that was not political.

3. What part do the common people have in this play of royalty and nobility?

Answer: One of Shakespeare's merits is his ability to convey the diversity and complexity of human experience. So here in a play which by its very nature must concern itself largely with a high-level ruling clique, Shakespeare introduces characters who occasionally expand our view to other segments of that world Richard II lived in. There are several references to the common people. The first comes from Richard as he describes vividly but with displeasure what he has heard about Bolingbroke's progress into exile. "The common people" lined Bolingbroke's route. There were craftsmen of various types, small-scale merchants and peddlers, like a woman who hawks oysters, and laborers, like the two draymen who shouted a "God speed" after Bolingbroke. This specifying of occupations takes us into the midst of this middle- and working-class group. We rub shoulders with them and for a while share their world, an effective change from the court atmosphere of most of the play. But this crowd has another important function. It reveals a further superiority of Bolingbroke over Richard. He knows how to charm the people and win them to his support, so he caters to this crowd; and York reports that he did the same in his triumphal return to London. Actually his true feeling about the common people may be the same as Richard's, who dismisses them as "slaves." But he knows their political value. Before the play is over, he is proved right and Richard wrong.

The conversation between Bagot, Bushy, and Green, when they realize the strength of Bolingbroke's rebellion, introduces another reference to the common people. This is a very brief passage, but it re-emphasizes Richard's failure with this group. In fact, they say the "commons" are filled with "deadly hate" for Richard because of the way in which he has emptied their purses. In less than a half-dozen lines Shakespeare makes us aware of the full dimensions of the society of the day and also its swelling discontent.

Three individual representatives of the common people play roles of some interest, even though they are of minor significance in the plot. At least two of them are attractive characters—attractive to the audience and sympathetic to Richard. Most interesting is the gardener at Langley. His allegory comparing England to a garden may be stiff and unlikely on the lips of a working man, but, nevertheless, this is a flesh and blood character who almost walks off the page. He is intent on his job, both as supervisor and actual worker; but he has interests beyond the horizon of his work; he is informed about the national situation. When challenged by the Queen, he sticks staunchly to his facts, but he amiably makes allowances for the Queen's frayed feelings. Perhaps we encounter here in this humble worker a compromise personality. He seems to have the imaginativeness and sensitivity of a Richard, and also the cool, efficient stability of a Bolingbroke. He operates in a lowly position in the ranks of the common people, but he brings to his little world a saneness and moderation that neither Richard nor Bolingbroke achieve for their worlds. The groom who appears in the next to the last scene is another representative of the common people. His contribution to the play is begun and ended in the short space of thirty lines. But we shall remember him. Like the gardener, he has that kind of complexity of nature which somehow makes a character seem human and credible. He has gone to some trouble to get permission to visit Richard. His motive seems to be sincere desire to see Richard—not morbid curiosity about the fallen King. But although so well-intentioned, he is not very sensitive and manages to make Richard unhappy by his reference to the favorite Barbary roan. He does truly pity Richard, however. Through his eyes we can see Richard's plight as it must seem to any ordinary mortal whose conscience has not been hardened and calloused by experience in the arena of power politics. The third individual is Richard's keeper or jailer. The development of his character is very limited. Richard calls him "a sad dog." If it was he who was playing the discordant music, he has some personal sympathy for the deposed king; but he is also easily used as a tool by Richard's enemies. The food he brings Richard is almost certainly poisoned, and he must know it. He deserves the drubbing Richard gives him. He and the two murdering thugs are wicked in their servile collaboration with the evil designs of the nobility.

The common people figure in the play both as a class and as individuals. As a class, they swell the anti-Richard forces in the basic political conflict. As individuals, they provide at least two convincing, if slight, sketches of human nature. Although this is primarily a play of the aristocracy, Shakespeare makes it more universal and realistic by suggesting the involvement of the whole nation—nobility and commoners—in the event.

4. Are Gaunt's speeches in Act 2, Scene 1, appropriate for a dying man?

Answer: For the first half of Act 2, Scene 1, John of Gaunt is on stage, conversing first with his brother York and then with his nephew Richard. He is close to death and does die a few minutes after he is borne off stage in mid-scene. His speeches are marked by strong emotion (anger with Richard) and by ornate language (plentiful imagery and clever wordplay). They include the best-known speech of the play, the long, loving description of England, "this dear dear land." They also include the punning on his own name, Gaunt.

Most listeners and readers find the high emotional pitch appropriate and believable. It is quite likely that a forceful man like Gaunt could summon us enough energy, even when dying, to reprove wrongdoing. In fact, the closeness of death would probably make him more intense and urgent; but the style of the speeches, it must be admitted, is not realistic. It is indeed unlikely that a mortally sick man, no matter how strong his patriotism, could invent that rosary of beautiful epithets for England: "royal throne of kings," "sceptered isle," "earth of majesty," "seat of Mars," "this other Eden," "demi-Paradise," and so on. It is even less likely that his mind would be sufficiently agile and sufficiently frivolous to want "to play so nicely" with words: "For sleeping England long time have I watched, / Watching breeds leanness, leanness is all gaunt . . . . / Gaunt am I for the grave, gaunt as a grave, / Whose hollow womb inherits naught but bones." Anyone who demands a photographic kind of realism will be unhappy with this scene. Shakespeare is experimenting with a heightened and more profound realism. It is true that he is not yet able to handle it with the artistry he was going to exhibit in his later plays, but he knows now what he wants to do. He wants to express not just what you would, in literal fact, hear the dying Gaunt say if you were beside him as he talks to York and Richard. He knows that he should, somehow, express what the dying Gaunt would want to say, what he would indeed *be* "saying" with his eyes, his facial expression, and his gestures. His great affection for England and the wry mockery behind the punning are just as real as the few broken sentences that the dying man would have strength to utter in real life. Shakespeare is trying to fulfill art's obligation to give total reality, not just the surface manifestations of it. He does not fully succeed here, partly because in this period, when he is infatuated with words, he believes that word cleverness alone can express the "specialness" of this deeper reality he is attempting to convey.

5. How does *Richard II* foreshadow the other plays in its tetralogy or set of four plays?

Answer: Shakespeare intended that *Richard II* would be the first in a set of four chronicle plays that would carry English history through approximately two decades from 1398 to 1421. The reigns of three kings are involved as the play's titles show: *Richard II, Henry IV, Part 1* and *Part 2, Henry V.* He wrote the plays in this order; but while he was composing *Richard II,* he was making his plans for the sequel plays. He was careful to establish links between the plays. In *Richard II* there are several passages that foreshadow events in the following plays. Some even project ahead into another tetralogy *(Henry VI, Part 1, Part 2* and *Part 3,* and *Richard III)* which covered the years 1422 to 1485.

The two Percy characters, father and son, are notable links between *Richard II* and the two parts of *Henry IV.* It is not merely that they reappear in the Henry plays. They change their political allegiance, and we are already being prepared for that change in *Richard II.* In this play they are, of course, staunch supporters of Bolingbroke. But the Earl of Northumberland and his son also are haughty and rather arrogant characters. They act chiefly for personal profit. When Henry IV (Bolingbroke) angers them, as he does early in his reign, they desert him and with strong allies raise an insurrection. This rift between Bolingbroke and the Percies is clearly foreshadowed early in Act 5 of *Richard II.* Richard warns the elder Northumberland, who stalks him like a sinister shadow through several scenes, that this fine alliance with Bolingbroke will not last. ". . . foul sin gathering head / Shall break into corruption. Thou shalt think, / Though he divide the realm and give thee half, / It is too little, helping him to all. / And he shall think that thou which know'st the way / To plant unrightful kings, will know again, . . . / To pluck him headlong from the usurped throne." The younger Percy, who is later to be called Hotspur, assures Bolingbroke of his continued service to him, when they first meet in the wilds of Gloucestershire. The foreshadowing here is ironic. Young Henry says to Bolingbroke, "I tender you my service, / Such as it is, being tender, raw and young, / Which elder days shall ripen and confirm / To more approved service and desert." Those elder days instead found Hotspur a fiery foe of Bolingbroke. In the actual fighting of the Percy insurrection, Hotspur is matched with Bolingbroke's son, Prince Hal. In *Richard II* there is already a coupling of their names and personalities. In the third scene of Act 5 the young Percy reports, rather self-righteously, Prince Hal's latest scandalous witticism. And here there is irony with a different accent. Although Hotspur and Hal were going to remain hostile, each would revise his opinion of the other before Hotspur's death under Hal's sword thrust. Hotspur would learn that Hal was not just a dissolute playboy; Hal would be moved to praise the rebel Hotspur: ". . . this earth that bears thee dead / Bears not alive so stout a gentleman."

Another important foreshadowing involves Prince Hal and his father. Young Percy tenders his information about Hal in Act 5, Scene 3, because Bolingbroke is worried about his madcap son. Harry Percy's report is just further evidence that Hal is leading a riotous life. But despite this, Bolingbroke clings to his belief that there are in his son "some sparks of better hope, which elder years / May happily bring forth." Both these aspects of Hal's character, the fun-loving irresponsibility and the basic integrity, are highlighted in the sequel plays of the tetralogy. He continues his wild life for a while, but gradually proves himself brave and noble, is reconciled with his father, and becomes the fine monarch Henry V, victor at Agincourt and the bluff, likable wooer of the charming French princess, Kate. At the end of *Richard II,* Bolingbroke vows that he will make a pilgrimage to Jerusalem to atone for his part in Richard's death. Part of his punishment is that he is never able to fulfill that vow and so get the satisfaction of atonement. It bothers his conscience all through *Henry IV, Part 1* and *Part 2*. At least three times in those plays he refers to this vow and his desire to make his "voyage to the Holy Land."

A more generalized but also more fundamental foreshadowing is provided by Carlisle's famous speech of prophecy in Act 4. His prediction of "tumultous wars," "disorder, horror, fear, and mutiny" is realized, not only in the remaining plays of this tetralogy, but even more emphatically and disastrously for England in the civil dissension and warring that flame all through the three parts of *Henry VI* and *Richard III*. Carlisle emphasizes that the family nature of the quarrel makes it more heinous. One grandson of Edward III, Bolingbroke, is offending another grandson, Richard. This family nature continues, and the Wars of the Roses and their aftermath in the reigns of Henry VI and Richard III are the same family quarrel several generations bitterer.

As an example of a very brief but effective link between *Richard II* and its sequel plays, we may remember the Queen's description of Richard as he approaches her while she waits on the street near the Tower of London. She calls him her "fair rose." In *Henry IV, Part 1,* young Harry Percy (Hotspur) angered now with Bolingbroke, regrets the deposition of "Richard, that sweet, lovely rose."

So, by various types of threads, Shakespeare weaves a connection between this prologue play and those that follow in its set. Most significant of all, of course, is the fact that the main action of *Richard II* produces the plots of the sequel plays. The decision to try to solve the problem presented by a weak king by replacing him with a stronger one was fatally productive of many other problems.

SUBJECT BIBLIOGRAPHY AND GUIDE TO RESEARCH PAPERS

The Tragedy of King Richard the Second has been edited many times, often by distinguished scholars. Especially useful for the student are the following editions: Matthew W. Black's New Variorum edition, published by Lippincott; Peter Ure's New Arden edition, published by Harvard University Press. Also to be recommended are Matthew W. Black's simpler edition, published by Penguin Books; G. B. Harrison's edition in his *Shakespeare: Major Plays*, published by Harcourt, Brace; George Lyman Kittredge's edition, published by Ginn; Kenneth Muir's Signet edition, published by New American Library; Robert T. Petersson's Yale edition, published by Yale University Press; J. Dover Wilson's New Cambridge edition, published by Cambridge University Press; Louis B. Wright and Virginia A. LaMar's Folger edition, published by Washington Square Press. Several of the above are available in paperback form. Interesting from the theatrical point of view is a 1958 edition published by the London Folio Society, *King Richard II*. Introduction by Sir John Gielgud.

The following is a selected list of works about Shakespeare and Richard II. They are arranged alphabetically by author and are subdivided according to the aspect of the play they discuss. For a more extensive list, the specialized Shakespeare bibliographies should be consulted. The most recent, in book form, is Gordon R. Smith's *A Classified Shakespeare Bibliography, 1936 to 1958*, published by Pennsylvania State University, in 1963.

BASIC WORKS

Adams, Joseph Q., *A Life of William Shakespeare*, New York: Houghton Mifflin, 1923. By common consensus one of the best biographical studies of Shakespeare.

Adams, Joseph Q., *Shakespearean Playhouses*, Gloucester: Peter Smith, 1960, reprint. Very readable account of the theaters of Shakespeare's time.

Bentley, Gerald E., *Shakespeare, A Biographical Handbook*, New Haven: Yale University Press, 1962. Paperback.

Bradley, A. C., *Shakespearean Tragedy*, New York: Meridian Books, 1955. Paperback. Excellent psychological studies of the four great tragic heroes and some incidental treatment of Shakespeare's other tragic figures.

Campbell, Lity B., *Shakespeare's "Histories," Mirrors of Elizabethan Policy*, San Marino: Huntington Library, 1947. The Elizabethan frame of reference for the politics in the chronicle plays.

Chambers, E. K., *Shakespeare: A Survey*, New York: Hill & Wang, 1958. Paperback. Brief informative essays on each of the plays.

Chute, Marchette, *Shakespeare of London*, New York: Dutton, 1957. Paperback. Good biographical and critical study. Popular in style but scholarly in its research.

Coleridge, Samuel T., *Shakespearean Criticism*, ed. by T. M. Raysor, Cambridge: Harvard University Press, 1930. One of the most original and sensitive of the early critics.

Dowden, Edward, *Shakespeare: A Critical Study of His Mind and Art*, New York: Putman, 1962. Paperback. Old-fashioned but still of value.

Granville-Barker, Harley and Harrison, G. B., eds., *A Companion to Shakespeare Studies*, New York: Doubleday Anchor, 1960. Paperback. Excellent set of essays by various experts in the Shakespearean field.

Hazlitt, William, *Characters of Shakespeare's Plays*, N. Y.: Dutton, 1906.

Johnson, Samuel, *Notes to Shakespeare*, Los Angeles: Clark Memorial Library, 1957. A good corrective to "bardolatry" by the "last and greatest Roman of them all."

Knight, G. Wilson, *The Imperial Theme*, London: Methuen, 1951. In final chapter, "The Prophetic Soul," treats Richard's prison soliloquy in its relation to Shakespeare's later works.

Spencer, Hazelton, *The Art and Life of William Shakespeare*, New York: Harcourt, Brace, 1940.

Tillyard, E. M. W., *The Elizabethan World Picture*, New York: Random House, n.d. Paperback. Explains Renaissance theory of man and the universe, and significance of the king in Elizabethan society.

Tillyard, E. M. W., *Shakespeare's History Plays*, New York: Collier Books, 1962. Paperback. A study of the plays as a Renaissance comment on the evils of political disorder.

Traversi, Derek A., *An Approach to Shakespeare,* New York: Doubleday Anchor, 1956. Paperback.
Traversi, Derek A., *Shakespeare: From Richard II to Henry V,* Palo Alto: Stanford University Press, 1957.

SOURCES AND HISTORICAL BACKGROUND OF RICHARD II

Questions to consider: What types of writing provided source material for *Richard II*? To what extent is Shakespeare indebted to his sources? How did he modify them and for what reasons? What similarities can be noted between Marlowe's *Edward II* and Shakespeare's *Richard II*? What is the basic political theory of the play? How does *Richard II* demonstrate the difference between the writing of history and the writing of poetic drama?

Black, Matthew W., "The Sources of Shakespeare's Richard II," Joseph Quincy Adams Memorial Studies, Ithaca: Cornell University Press, pp. 199-216.
Bullough, Geoffrey, ed., *Narrative and Dramatic Sources of Shakespeare,* Vol. 3, New York: Columbia University Press, 1958.
Daniel, Samuel, *The Civil Wars,* ed. L. Michel, New Haven: Yale University Press, 1958.
Dean, Leonard, F., "Richard II: The State and the Image of the Theater," *Publications of the Modern Language Association,* vol. 67 (1952), pp. 211-218.
Marlowe, Christopher, *Edward II,* San Francisco: Chandler, 1961. Paperback.
Marriott, J. A. R., *English History in Shakespeare,* New York: Dutton, 1918.
McKisack, May, *The Fourteenth Century,* Oxford: Clarendon Press, 1959.
Nicoll, A. and J., eds., *Holinshed's Chronicles as Used in Shakespeare's Plays,* New York: Dutton, 1927.
Palmer, John, *Political Characters in Shakespeare,* New York: Macmillan, 1945. Also published, two volumes in one, as *Political and Comic Characters of Shakespeare,* New York: St. Martin's Library, 1962.
Rossiter, A. P., ed., *Woodstock: A Moral History,* London: Chatto & Windus, 1946.
Smith, R. M., *Froissart and the English Chronicle Play,* New York: Columbia University Press, 1915.
Wilson, John D., "The Political Background of Shakespeare's Richard II and Henry IV," *Shakespeare-Jahrbuch,* vol. 75 (1939), pp. 36-51.

CONNECTION OF THE PLAY WITH THE ESSEX CONSPIRACY

Questions to consider: Why did this play have topical significance for the Elizabethans? How did the Essex conspirators use this play and other literature as propaganda? Why and how did its political experience influence the early printings of the play?

Albright, Evelyn M., "Richard II, Hayward's History of Henry IV and the Essex Conspiracy," *Publications of the Modern Language Association,* vol. 46 (1931), pp. 694-719.

Albright, Evelyn M., "Shakespeare's Richard II and the Essex Conspiracy," *Publications of the Modern Language Association*, vol. 42 (1927), pp. 686-720.
Black, John B., *The Reign of Elizabeth*, Oxford: Clarendon, 1959.
Cheyney, Edward P., *A History of England from the Defeat of the Armada to the Death of Elizabeth*, London: Longmans, Green, 1914-1926.
Harrison, G. B., *The Life and Death of Robert Devereux, Earl of Essex*, New York: Holt, 1937.
Heffner, R., "Shakespeare, Hayward and Essex," *Publications of the Modern Language Association*, vol. 45 (1930), pp. 754-780.
Kuhl, E. P., "Shakespeare and Hayward," *Studies in Philology*, Vol. 25 (1928), pp. 312-315.
Shakespeare, William, *The Tragedy of King Richard II*, printed . . . in 1598, reproduction in facsimile, with introduction by Alfred W. Pollard, London: Quaritch, 1916.
Strachey, Giles, *Elizabeth and Essex, a Tragic History*, New York: Harcourt, Brace, 1928.

CHARACTERIZATION OF RICHARD

Questions to consider: Is Shakespeare successful in this characterization? What type of person does Shakespeare consider Richard to be? How does Richard compare with Shakespeare's other tragic heroes? How does the characterization compare with recent biographical and dramatic treatments of the King? Is Shakespeare partisan in his treatment of Richard?

Campbell, Lily, *Shakespeare's Tragic Heroes*, New York: Barnes and Noble, 1959. Paperback.
Craig, Hardin, "Shakespeare's Development as a Dramatist in the Light of His Experience," *Studies in Philology*, vol. 39 (1942), pp. 226-238.
Draper, John W., "The Character of Richard II," *Philological Quarterly*, vol. 21 (1942), pp. 228-236.
Hutchinson, Harold F., *The Hollow Crown Life of Richard II*, New York: John Day, 1961.
Mackintosh, Elizabeth (Gordon Daviot, pseud.), *Richard of Bordeaux*, Boston: Little, Brown, 1933. A play.
McPeek, James, "Richard and His Shadow World," *American Imago*, vol. 15 (1958), pp. 195-212.
Palmer, John, *Political Characters of Shakespeare*, New York: Macmillan, 1945.
Quinn, Michael, " 'The King Is Not Himself': The Personal Tragedy of Richard II," *Studies in Philology*, vol. 56 (1959), pp. 169-186.
Reese, Max M., *The Cease of Majesty*, New York: St. Martin's Press, 1962.
Rossiter, A. P., *Angel with Horns*, New York: Theatre Arts Books, 1961.
Steel, Anthony, *Richard II*, Cambridge:Cambridge University Press, 1963.
Swinburne, A. C., *Three Plays of Shakespeare*, New York: Harper, 1909.
Thompson, Karl F., "Richard II, Martyr," *Shakespeare Quarterly*, Vol. 8 (1957), pp. 159-166.
Yeats, W. B., *Ideas of Good and Evil*, New York: Macmillan, 1903.

OTHER CHARACTERIZATIONS

Questions to consider: To what extent is Bolingbroke a foil character for Richard? To what extent is Bolingbroke admirable? Objectionable? Is Shakespeare partisan in his treatment of Bolingbroke? Is this a one-character play? Are there inconsistencies in the characterization?

Dodson, Sarah C., "The Northumberland of Shakespeare and Holinshed," *Texas Studies in English*, vol. 19 (1939), pp. 74-85.

Kleinstuck, Johannes, "The Character of Henry Bolingbroke," *Neophilologus*, vol. 41 (1957), pp. 51-56.

Ribner, Irving, "Bolingbroke, a True Machiavellian," *Modern Language Quarterly*, vol. 9 (1948), pp. 117-184.

Stirling, Brents, "Bolingbroke's 'Decision'," *Shakespeare Quarterly*, vol. 3 (1952), pp. 27-34.

Taylor, M. P., "A Father Pleads for the Death of His Son," *International Journal of Psycho-Analysis*, vol. 8 (1927), pp. 53-55.

IMAGERY AND OTHER STYLISTIC ELEMENTS

Questions to consider: What images recur in the play? What is their significance? What makes this one of the most poetic of Shakespeare's plays? Does Shakespeare the poet frustrate Shakespeare the dramatist in this play?

Altick, Richard D., "Symphonic Imagery in Richard II," *Publications of the Modern Language Association*, vol. 62 (1947), pp. 339-365.

Bryant, J. A., Jr., "The Linked Analogies of Richard II," *Sewanee Review*, vol. 75 (1957), pp. 420-433.

Cauthen, I. B., Jr., "Richard II and the Image of the Betrayed Christ," *Renaissance Papers*, (1954), pp. 45-48.

Clemen, Wolfgang H., *The Development of Shakespeare's Imagery*, Cambridge: Harvard University Press, 1951.

Doran, Madeleine, "Imagery in Richard II and in Henry IV," *Modern Language Review*, vol. 37 (1942), pp. 113-122.

Halliday, F. E., *The Poetry of Shakespeare's Plays*, London: Duckworth, 1954.

Heninger, S. K., Jr., "The Sun-King Analogy in Richard II," *Shakespeare Quarterly*, vol. 11 (1960), pp. 319-327.

Kliger, Samuel, "The Sun Imagery in Richard II," *Studies in Philology*, vol. 45 (1948), pp. 196-202.

Mahood, M. M., *Shakespeare's Word Play*, London: Methuen, 1956.

Saintsbury, George, *A History of English Prosody from the Twelfth Century to the Present Day*, vol. 2, pp. 3-204, 2d ed., New York: Macmillan, 1923.

Spurgeon, Caroline F. E., *Shakespeare's Imagery, and What It Tells Us*, Boston: Beacon Press, 1958. Paperback. The classic book for this material.

Stauffer, Donald A., *Shakespeare's World of Images*, New York: Norton, 1949.

Suzman, Arthur, "Imagery and Symbolism in Richard II," *Shakespeare Quarterly*, vol. 7 (1956), pp. 355-370.

Van Doren, Mark, *Shakespeare*, New York: Doubleday Anchor, 1953. Paperback.